May 1901, three ...
...rse-drawn sledge to bring back what rema...
of the huge beast. The hunters had
...ken the tusks to sell in a nearby city, but th...
...f the animal was still completely entombe...
...e earth and ice, its massive body frozen soli...
had to be thawed, cut into pieces, refroze...
and hauled out from the steppes
on a train of sledges.

These photographs are from the book
published in 1926 by E. W. Pfizenmayer, one of the
three scientists of the expedition. An English edition
Mammoths and Man in Siberia
was published in 1939.

CONTENTS

THE STORY OF FOSSILS
IN SEARCH OF VANISHED WORLDS

Yvette Gayrard-Valy

THAMES AND HUDSON

Relatively new links in the vast chain of living things, human beings have always had intuitive feelings about the remains of the life-forms that preceded them. Chance finds of odd-looking objects on pathside or beach fired their imagination and inspired legends about gods, devils and monsters.

CHAPTER 1
MYTHS AND LEGENDS

Beyond death, traces of life: sand turned into stone and entombed this fish (opposite) for all time. Right: reconstruction of a Neanderthal.

How far back can we trace human interest in fossils? Judging from a collection of fossil gastropods (a class of molluscs) and corals found in a cave in Burgundy, France, probably to the very dawn of humankind. To whom did these fossils belong? Presumably to the Neanderthal – or group of Neanderthals – believed to have lived in this cave eighty thousand years ago. How did the Neanderthals discover these fossils? Perhaps on their way back from hunting, or while gathering fruit, or in the course of a migration in search of food – by chance. And so it would be for their distant descendants. The development of technical and scientific tools for systematic fossil hunting is a recent phenomenon. Before these innovations people came across fossils purely by accident, while they were out walking, or quarrying rock, or digging during construction or roadwork.

Imagine the moment a fossil caught the eye of our Neanderthal. Perhaps it was a stone unlike any other, one that recalled an animal seen somewhere else before, or maybe it seemed totally unfamiliar. And usually there was not just one – these rocks seemed always to occur in clusters, in what came to be known as deposits. At any rate, these stones were intriguing. The Neanderthal picked them up and soon started to collect them. Why? Simply because they were beautiful? Did early humans endow the fossils with magical or religious powers? Although we can conjecture, we cannot know the answer.

Grimaldi (Italy), Dunstable Down (England), Issoire (France): these are names that hark back to the earliest chapters in the history of humankind. Here and in other prehistoric sites sea urchins, ammonites, seashells and shark teeth have been discovered – all of them fossils, many perforated as if to be worn as amulets. In Egypt fossils were found at what are believed to be Neolithic localities; there, as early as the dynastic period (c. 3200–c. 343 BC) some fossils were being set in metal.

A 35,000-year-old fossil-shell necklace from Cro-Magnon (post-Neanderthal) times (left) and a 10,000-year-old Neolithic anthropomorphic figurine of fossil-bearing marble (below) attest to the presence of fossils in even the remotest periods of human history.

In 1875 the skeletons of an old woman and a young man, together with some chipped flint implements, were discovered in the Grotta dei Fanciulli (Cave of the Children) at Grimaldi, in northwest Italy (left and detail above). Lying side by side, legs sharply bent, they bear red markings and several rows of small fossil gastropods around the head and hip. The grave dates from Late Palaeolithic times, and these are fossils of *Homo sapiens,* our distant cousins who lived at the end of the fourth Ice Age. At this time – 35,000 years ago – mammoths, reindeer, and saiga antelope (sheeplike antelope of Siberia and eastern Russia) freely roamed the steppes and tundra, and humans sought the protection of caves and rock shelters.

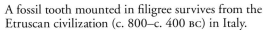

A fossil tooth mounted in filigree survives from the Etruscan civilization (c. 800–c. 400 BC) in Italy.

Restless realm of the gods, the skies of classical antiquity yield a bounty of fossils

According to Roman scholar Pliny the Elder (AD 23–79), shark teeth were popularly believed to be petrified tongues that fell from the sky during eclipses of the moon. He called them *glossopetrae* (tongue stones) because of their supposed resemblance to the tongues of snakes, and the name stuck until the 17th century. The shells of sea urchins were often said to be stones that fell to earth when it thundered or rained. Pliny, however, speculated that they were 'turtle hatchlings turned into stone' or magic snake eggs. As he noted, 'These eggs are prized by the druids, who believe them to be a most effective way to ensure favourable reception by princes.'

The heavens were also said to provide us with amber, translucent fossilized tree resin. Or was it, as some contended, congealed wildcat urine (dark for males, fainter for females)? Condensed 'moisture from the sun's rays'? Tears shed by guinea fowl or by Phaëthon's grieving sisters, who were turned into poplar trees after he was killed by a thunderbolt? Solidified sea foam? Some called it *electrum* (from Elector, a Greek name for the sun), Pliny called it *succinum,* from the Latin word for 'sap.' Although it later became apparent that amber is in fact created by plants, people clung to the belief that it was melted by the sun's rays and hardened by the sea.

'Horns of Ammon are shaped like inwardly coiling ram's horns, and some appear to be clad in golden armour'

The whorled structure of ammonites (the fossil shells of extinct cephalopods) inspired the name 'horns of Ammon', after an Egyptian deity represented as having ram's horns. Magicians availed themselves of ammonites to conjure up 'divine visions during sleep'. In the Middle Ages they were thought to be headless snakes coiling around their tails; in both Germany and England they were commonly known as snake stones. According to a legend associated with the town of

According to legend, St Hilda, an Anglo-Saxon abbess, planned to found a monastery near Whitby in Yorkshire, but the place was rumoured to be cursed and was overrun by little snakes. The abbess is said to have beheaded them all and turned them to stone.

This skilfully executed forgery would convince anyone that ammonites always had snakes' heads.

F ossil shells from Mesozoic times (225 to 65 million years ago), ammonites were so named because of their resemblance to the coiled horns of Ammon, the ram-headed deity of ancient Egypt (left).

Whitby, in Yorkshire, ammonites were vestiges of the little snakes that the abbess St Hilda (614–80) had beheaded and turned into stone. To keep the story fresh in people's minds, local ammonite gatherers sold 'restored' snakes, complete with 'reattached' hand-carved heads!

These are but a few of the countless attempts to make sense of fossils.

The remains of large vertebrates inspire legends about human giants, mythical monsters, and terrifying animals

Perhaps as long as five thousand years ago, probably while exploring a cave at the foot of Mount Etna in Sicily, Achaean sailors from ancient Greece discovered some remains that looked like human bones, only huge. How frightened they must have been! They also found a skull, then another – just as big, just as forbidding – with a single ominous socket in the middle of the forehead. No question but that the bones belonged to gigantic humans,

R ecalling the legend of St Hilda, snake-headed ammonites emblazon the coat of arms of the town of Whitby.

appalling one-eyed monsters which probably dwelled on the island and whose burial place the sailors had unwittingly desecrated. Best to clear out posthaste and move on! When these sailors spun their tales to their friends and families back home, conjuring up visions of fearsome creatures, their listeners took heart from the sure knowledge that the discoveries were so far away.

Centuries went by, and the stories were passed along from generation to generation. In the 5th century BC Greek historian Thucydides asserted that Cyclopia, the mythical land of the Cyclopes – where the hapless Ulysses looked on as Poseidon's son, the Cyclops Polyphemus, devoured several of his shipmates – lay on the slopes of Mount Etna. This view was corroborated by his contemporary, the philosopher Empedocles, of Agrigentum. But they were both off the mark. Cyclopia – that is, the land of the giants described by Homer – lay more to the north, near Naples. More importantly, however, their assertions perpetuated a widely held belief. The idea that there really were such things as Cyclopes went unchallenged for centuries, and they were joined by many other giants. In Pliny we read that the skeleton of the mythological hunter Orion, 26 cubits (about 23 metres) long, was discovered on the island of Crete. The remains of Trojan War hero Ajax were said to have been discovered at Salamis, an ancient city on the east coast of Cyprus. The Arabs, too, acknowledged belief in the existence of human giants. During the Middle Ages and the Renaissance, the hold of myths about giants was stronger than ever. From a catalogue compiled in 1558, we know that between the 14th and 16th centuries quite a few bones of 'giants' were still turning up in Sicily.

The creatures people used to call Cyclopes really did exist, only hundreds of thousands of years earlier than

❝ We…reached the country of the lawless outrageous Cyclopes [shown in a mask, left, and in a 16th-century engraving, opposite] who, putting all their trust in the immortal gods, neither plough with their hands nor plant anything.… When we had arrived at the place, which was nearby, there at the edge of the land we saw the cave, close to the water, high and overgrown with laurels, and in it were stabled great flocks, sheep and goats alike, and there was a fenced yard built around it with a high wall of…boulders and tall pines and oaks with lofty foliage. Inside there lodged a monster of a man, who now was herding the flocks at a distance away, alone, for he did not range with others, but stayed away by himself; his mind was lawless, and in truth he was a monstrous wonder made to behold, not like a man, an eater of bread, but more like a wooded peak of the high mountains seen standing away from the others.❞

Homer
Odyssey, Book IX

had been thought; so did the closely related giants whose bones had been unearthed at various other sites. Contrary to legend – and their huge molars notwithstanding – they had, however, never tasted the tiniest morsel of human flesh. In fact, they were vegetarians! And they all had small, round, peaceful eyes – not one, but two of them. The baffling forehead socket turned out to be a large median nasal opening that boasted a trunk when the creatures were alive. The creatures were in reality harmless dwarf elephants that roamed the islands of the Mediterranean early in the Quaternary period, over 1.5 million years ago.

By the time humans stumbled upon their remains, these elephants had all died out – as had their cousins throughout Europe. The bones were real enough; the human giants they supposedly belonged to, however, were figments of the imagination.

'Now tell me, whatever could I have been?'

Stories about giants, monsters and other mythical beings continued to be told all over Europe for centuries, some until fairly recently. In the 1st century AD Plutarch speculated that some bones found on the Aegean island of Samos belonged to Amazons slain by Dionysus. In the 17th century, the supposed grave of Theutobochus, 'king of the Cimbri' (an early Germanic tribe), was discovered in southeastern France, and the bones of Alaric and his Visigoth warriors were found in the Pyrenees. (In every case, remains of large vertebrates.) Apparently, the giants had been defeated: that was some comfort.

An angel fallen from heaven, or a giant six metres tall? That was the question everyone in 16th-century

Switzerland was asking when some bones were found near the abbey of Renden. The consensus was that it was a giant, and a picture of it was painted on the tower of the city hall. Around the same time, in the town of Schwäbisch-Hall in southwestern Germany, a mammoth tusk was displayed along with some verse:

On the 13th of February
In the year sixteen hundred and five,
I was found near Neubronn, in the vicinity of Hall.
Now tell me, whatever could I have been?

Perhaps the bone belonged to a saint! In a similar instance, a mammoth molar and an

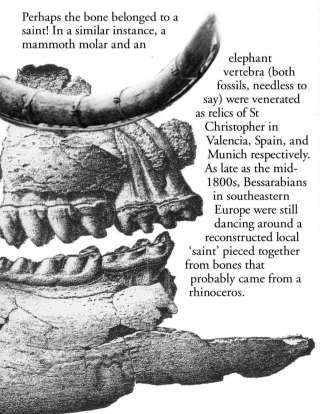

elephant vertebra (both fossils, needless to say) were venerated as relics of St Christopher in Valencia, Spain, and Munich respectively. As late as the mid-1800s, Bessarabians in southeastern Europe were still dancing around a reconstructed local 'saint' pieced together from bones that probably came from a rhinoceros.

Large, now-extinct mammals once roamed Europe and the shores of the Mediterranean Sea. The most spectacular group, the proboscideans, included giant species during the Cenozoic era, which began about 65 million years ago. The Deinotheriidae stood 4 metres tall at the withers and wielded a single pair of tusks directed down from the lower jaw. Mastodons (left, below), armed with both upper and lower sets of tusks, died out at the dawn of the Quaternary (more than 1.5 million years ago); whereas mammoths (left, above), with their upwardly curved upper tusks, did not appear until then, meaning that they coexisted with Neanderthals. The discovery of whole mammoth carcasses, shaggy fur and all, in the permafrost of Siberiacleared the way for accurate reconstructions.

Dragons, unicorns, and giant rats take their places in legend and lore

Looking for all the world like an archetypal dragon, a stone monster carved between the late 16th and early 17th centuries dominates a square in the southern Austrian town of Klagenfurt. Another figment of the imagination? Not quite. Its head was modelled after a skull that had been found about 1335 and displayed in the town hall. It actually belonged to a woolly rhinoceros that had died tens of thousands of years earlier. Since the creature was presumed to be the dragon of a local legend, it was only natural for the sculptor to incorporate its supposed 'likeness' into his work. According to Othenio Abel, a palaeontologist active in the first half of the 20th century, Klagenfurt's dragon fountain was the earliest palaeontological reconstruction.

Meanwhile, articles about dragons started to appear in scholarly journals. The Kaiserliche Leopoldinische Akademie, a German society of scholars, reported that in 1672–3 dragon bones had been found in caves in the Carpathian mountains of Transylvania, in western Romania. We can tell from the drawings accompanying the article that the creature was actually a cave bear.

Also in the 17th century the partial skeleton of a dragon said to have been slain by a young hero (according to a local legend that thrilled fireside listeners in rural areas as recently as the early 1900s) was found near Mixnitz in the Austrian province of Styria. It, too, turned out to belong to a cave bear.

In China, however, dragons were benevolent creatures beloved by farmers – they supposedly caused the rain to fall. The gigantic teeth and bones scattered here and there were thought by the Chinese to belong to dragons that had been unable to find a cloud to fly back into.

In Siberia, mammoth skeletons perpetuated the legend of huge, buffalo-sized rodents that lived underground, burrowed into rock or wood, and died when exposed to the light of the sun or the moon. The earth shook whenever the rodents moved about. Charles Darwin found similar myths existing in South America as recently as the middle of the 19th century.

Supposedly 'begotten by Satan to vie with God', fossilized creatures were often pictured alongside the goats and magic potions traditionally associated with witchcraft (above).

Chinese dragons (left, below) had horns, claws, scales and barbed tails, but they used their power – which was thought to come from a pearl held in their mouth – to do good. Dragons, monsters and giants have held all civilizations spellbound at one time or another. Invariably evil, European dragons were usually represented as large, fearsome, fire-spitting, smoke-belching reptiles with claws and wings. Fortunately, heroes like Hercules, St Michael, and St George came along to slay them. According to Navaho legend, the huge silicified tree trunks scattered across Arizona are the remains of Yetso, a monstrous giant their ancestors had to slay when they first settled in the region. In other tribal legends, the trees are the shafts of arrows loosed by a thunder god or shattered weapons that fell to earth as gods and giants did battle.

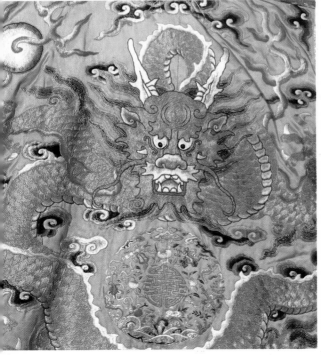

Some of the fossil tusks or horns of large extinct mammals, it was said, came from unicorns, a myth that probably originated in the East and was closely associated with the Indian rhinoceros.

The 'Balm of Europe'

Anselmus Boetius de Boodt, court physician to Holy Roman Emperor Rudolf II (1552–1612), gave an extensive rundown of fossils' purported attributes in *Parfaict Ioailler ou Histoire des Pierreries* (The History of Precious Stones), 1644. Some of these 'virtues' went unchallenged until not so very long ago and are still credited in certain quarters to this day.

Sea urchins were said to offer protection from lightning, venom and poisons. On certain islands in northern Scotland, ammonites – known locally as 'crampstones' – were thought to cure cramps in cows; the affected area was washed with water in which the stones had been left to steep for several hours.

Thought to be magic snake eggs, sea urchin shells were gathered, according to Pliny, because of their alleged power to 'ensure favourable reception by princes.' Left: a medieval woodcut.

A winged ant caught in a piece of amber forty million years ago (left).

Coveted by apothecaries, belemnites (the conical shells of extinct cephalopods, a type of mollusc) were used to treat nightmares, heal sores, cure pleurisy and cleanse the teeth. To rid them of parasites, horses were made to drink

water in which a belemnite had been soaked. Belemnites were also recommended for rheumatism and eye injuries. To treat the latter – in both humans and horses – fossils were ground into a fine powder and blown into the eyes.

Amber was administered in powder form, in an oil base, or as a sweetmeat; it was also worn as an amulet, a practice that has survived down to the 20th century. To quote one chronicler, amber was 'good for watery eyes, the heart, diseases of the brain, shortness of breath, the stone, dropsy, dysentery, toothache, menses, childbirth, gout, epilepsy, catarrh, aching joints, the stomach, plague, night fright...; it neutralizes poison and may be worn as an amulet to ward off spells,' and brings down a fever. In short, 'so wonderful are its powers that it can rightly be called the Balm of Europe.'

Pulverized shark teeth – the celebrated *glossopetrae* – were considered an effective remedy for snakebite, vomiting, fever and spells. Or a whole tooth could be worn as an amulet. Tongue-stones' reputed power to neutralize poison earned little tree-shaped tongue-stone holders a place of honour on European dining tables from the Middle Ages to the 18th century.

Popularly thought to be stones that grew in toads' heads, bufonites – actually fossilized fish teeth – were believed to hold magical powers. Left: a woodcut showing a bufonite being used as a cure.

Prized antidotes during the Middle Ages, a time when people were obsessed with poison, *glossopetrae* suspended from 'tongue-stone trees' were a fixture on banquet tables. A number of these are superb examples of precious metalwork (below).

Chinese pharmacologists have for centuries made extensive use of fossils. One 18th-century Chinese medical treatise attributed countless healing properties to 'dragon' bones, teeth, and horns. Ingested raw, fried in oil, cooked in rice wine or administered as a powder, they were touted as a veritable panacea, good for everything from constipation and heart or liver complaints to nightmares and epilepsy.

In the 19th and early 20th centuries, Chinese apothecaries were of great help to European palaeontologists, who first found fossilized mammal remains on drugstore shelves. Although many of the specimens were in poor condition and provided the scientists with few clues as to their geographical origin, they were welcome additions to scientific collections and, like fossils elsewhere, contributed to a better understanding of the evolution of life on our planet.

Unicorn horn (above left) – in fact, the fossilized tusks of elephants, rhinoceroses, and narwhals – was hailed as a miracle drug. In 1700 a royal pharmacy in Germany purchased sixty such 'horns'.

A epyornis maximus, a giant bird 2.70 metres tall, lived in Madagascar during the Quaternary, coexisting with the earliest humans. Greek historian Herodotus (5th century BC), Venetian traveller Marco Polo (1254–1324) and Persian legends helped rescue it from oblivion, if not extinction.

❝ The sun was about to set. Suddenly, the sky grew dark as if veiled by a thick cloud. Astonished as I was by this darkness, I marvelled even more when I saw that the cloud was a bird of inordinate length and girth. It was flying in my direction. I recalled often hearing sailors speak of a bird known as the roc, and I realized that the great dome I was marvelling at must be one of the bird's eggs. I was right: the mother roc was about to alight and settle on the egg to brood. As she swooped down, I huddled close to the egg; now I had before me a bird's foot as big as a stout tree trunk. I lashed myself to it.... When dawn broke, the roc took wing, lifting me to such heights that I could no longer see the earth.❞
Thousand and One Nights

Humans puzzled over the history of the world

Preposterous though they may seem, these beliefs must be recognized as attempts to fathom the meaning of natural phenomena. Ignorance may for a time have prevented humans from seeing fossils for what they really were, but it never hindered their attempts to fit fossils into their surroundings and history.

It fell to scholars and scientists to account for the vestiges of the past in an objective, rational way. It would prove a challenging task, full of missteps and misgivings.

Left: a 17th-century engraving of a winged dragon.

Scholars and scientists forged ahead even as the popularity of legends about these mystifying fossils grew. Yet, for all the speculation and hypotheses, the secrets of these stones' true identity and age would not be unlocked for a long time to come.

CHAPTER 2
THE QUEST FOR MEANING

Fossils appeared in books, filled private curio collections, such as the one depicted opposite, and for some became a virtual obsession. Right: a 17th-century engraving of a collector.

Some of the ancient Greek scientists had seen things as they really were. The earliest objective descriptions of fossils and general commentaries on the subject can be traced back to the 6th century BC. According to Anaximander (610–c. 547 BC), Pythagoras (c. 580–c. 500 BC), Xenophanes (c. 560–c. 478 BC) and Herodotus, the stone shells and fish imprints they had occasion to observe were the remains of organisms that once lived in the sea. If such remains were found inland, they reasoned, it was because land now dry was once covered by water.

Thus the one and only correct theory – that fossils are the remains of organisms that lived in very different conditions a long, long time ago – had already been put forward; but Aristotle, in the 4th century BC, took a different view. Arguing from the premise of spontaneous generation, he maintained that fossils were produced by 'vaporous exhalations' deep inside the earth – a hypothesis that would be invoked repeatedly throughout the Middle Ages and even later.

Roman commentators such as Lucretius, Horace, and Ovid – all of the 1st century BC – echoed the thinking of the Greeks. However, as Pliny the Elder's *Historia Naturalis* (Natural History) proves time and again, the siren call of legend was hard to resist.

Science versus theology: where did fossils fit in?

In the early Middle Ages (from roughly 500 to 900) the schools of the Roman Empire had vanished. Education – a rudimentary one at that – was reserved for prospective clergymen, and monasteries wholly oriented towards religion emerged as the new hubs of cultural life.

The resurgence of cities and the organization of student and faculty guilds into universities in the late 12th and early 13th centuries fostered an intellectual rebirth, but knowledge of fossils remained virtually

At the dawn of the Christian era, Greek geographer Strabo set forth a plausible explanation for the occurrence of fossils well inland from the sea. The seafloor, he argued, is not stable: 'The same bed sometimes rises, sometimes falls, now lifting, now lowering the level of the sea; and when it rises, adjoining land areas are inundated....' Pliny's *Historia Naturalis,* on the other hand, contained more popular beliefs and superstitions regarding fossils. Left: a page from a 15th-century edition of Pliny's work is at left.

Throughout the Middle Ages, manuscripts disseminated the writings of classical authors. Pictured left is an illustration from Franciscan friar Bartholomew the Englishman's *De Proprietatibus Rerum* (On the Properties of Things), first printed in 1495, more than two hundred years after his death.

unchanged. The curricula of the universities were predicated on the Holy Scriptures and the church fathers. Science was an integral part of theology. Questions concerning the origin of the universe were referred to the Bible, which set forth the cause and chronology of all events: where the universe came from, how the plant and animal worlds were created, and how humankind came to populate the earth.

Anyone straying from established dogma courted excommunication, an ecclesiastical sentence tantamount

In the 13th century the University of Paris emerged as a focal point of all then-known intellectual disciplines. Its general curriculum embraced each branch of knowledge, secular and religious alike. There were four faculties at the university: theology, medicine, religious law and the arts. The school of the arts – roughly equivalent to present-day secondary schools – grounded students in the liberal arts (grammar, logic, rhetoric, arithmetic, geometry, astronomy and music). Observation and experimentation were nonexistent. Students read and learned by rote classical writings, notably those of Aristotle.

A 13th-century depiction of life at school, left.

to being cast out from society. Several centuries were to
elapse before science finally disengaged itself from
theological studies.

The Renaissance witnesses the emergence of an intellectual elite with a passion for natural objects, a trend that is to prove increasingly popular in the centuries to come

Now the intelligentsia expanded to include laypeople
and the clergy alike. The scholar of the day – often a
combination of physician, astronomer, mathematician
and engineer who might also dabble in the highly
profitable fields of alchemy and magic –
gained unprecedented respect. Patrons
took scholars under their wing and made
it financially possible for them to
devote all their time to observation,
study and speculation. In turn,
scholars attracted pupils and
disciples. A new breed of amateur
scholar who travelled, corresponded
with fellow intellectuals on a wide
range of subjects and disseminated
new theories was born. This process was
abetted by the invention of the printing
press and the development of inexpensive
rag paper late in the 15th century.
The natural sciences enjoyed an
extraordinary surge in popularity. As
more and more 'oddities' turned up,
individuals started building highly eclectic
collections of 'curiosities'. Fossils – at the time,
anything dug out of the ground, including organic
remains, 'petrifactions', minerals, even prehistoric tools –
were displayed alongside paintings, pieces of sculpture,
crystals and other concretions, mounted animal
specimens (some genuine curiosities, others forgeries
pieced together from odds and ends) and skeletons of
every description.

Scholars recorded the contents of these collections
in catalogues. The first such published compilation
(1561) was followed by a pioneering catalogue of a

MUSEI
WORMIANI
HISTORIA
LUGD BATAVORUM
EX OFFICINA ELSEVIRIANA

Curiosities were the pride and joy of the nobility, and small fortunes were spent amassing collections (left above, a 17th-century engraving). In Germany and at the Hapsburg court of Austria, collecting was a prerogative of kings and princes. This craze peaked in the 18th century: the city of Paris alone boasted seventeen private collections in 1742, twenty-one in 1757, and sixty in 1780. The most famous was the one the wealthy Joseph Bonnier de la Mosson put on display in his sumptuous mansion (now the Hôtel de Lude). A number of these collections would evolve into museums.

During the Middle Ages and the Renaissance, the worlds of magic and science overlapped considerably. Since most scholar-scientists (left below) practised alchemy and astrology with great conviction, people believed they possessed mysterious powers, and high-ranking officials often sought their advice.

An illustration from a treatise written by Fabio Colonna in 1616, opposite.

fossil collection in Saxony compiled by Conrad Gesner (1516–65). Michele Mercati (1541–93), director of the Vatican botanical garden, catalogued the fossils, prehistoric tools, and important mineralogical specimens that made the collection of Pope Sixtus V one of the finest of its day. Mercati's 1574 *Metallotheca Vaticana* (Metals of the Vatican), however, did not appear in print until 1719. A mineralogist from Bologna, Ulisse Aldrovandi (1522–1605), catalogued his own collection, including vertebrate fossils, in 87 manuscript volumes, but the work, the *Musaeum Metallicum* (Museum of Metals), was not published until 1648.

Scientific journals came into their own throughout Europe in the 17th century: The first issues of *Le Journal des Savants* and *Philosophical Transactions of the Royal Society* appeared in France and England respectively in 1665. Court 'menageries' gave way to true zoological gardens. The popularization of science among intellectuals had begun. From then on, advances in sciences were made not only through the dissemination of knowledge, but through active cooperation between scientists of different nationalities and between professionals and amateurs.

ARCA RERVM FOSSI-lium Ioan. Kentmani.	
1 TERRAE	2 SVCCI NATIVI.
3 EFFLORESCENTES	4 PINGVES
5 LAPIDES	6 LAPID. IN ANIMALIBVS
7 FLVORES	8 SILICES
9 GEMMAE	10 MARMORA
11 SAXA	12 LIGNA IN Saxa corporata.
13 ARENAE	14 AVRVM
15 ARGENTVM	16 ARGENTVM VIVVM
17 AES SEV CVPRVM	18 CADMIA MET. PLVMBAGO
19 PYRITES	20 PLVMBVM NIGRVM
21 CINEREVM	22 CANDIDVM
23 STIBI	24 FERRVM
25 STOMOMA	26 MARINA VARIA

Quicquid terra sinus, venisq; recondidit imis,
Thesaurus orbis hac brevis arca tegit.
Iam magna est tacitas naturæ inquirere vires,
Maior in hoc ipsum munere nosse Deum.
Georg. Fabricius. C.

B orn in Zurich in 1516, Conrad Gesner won acclaim for his writings on zoology and botany. In *De Omni Rerum Fossilium* (A Book on Fossil Objects), 1565, he classified all kinds of objects that had been dug out of the earth, assigning each of the specimens (which he called 'fossils') a place in a numbered 'drawer' and providing a corresponding list of contents (left).

Schooled in mathematics, Latin, law, philosophy and medicine, Ulisse Aldrovandi, one of the most brilliant scholar-scientists of the Italian Renaissance, taught logic and natural history at the University of Bologna. He had his differences with the Church but enjoyed the protection of Pope Gregory XIII, whose financial support enabled him to dedicate himself to his prolific writings on natural history, including *Musaeum Metallicum,* illustrated by the author. Detail of the title page, left, and drawing of a fossil, below. Aldrovandi also founded Bologna's botanical garden.

The intelligentsia consider it fashionable to speculate about the origin of fossils, which leads to plenty of far-fetched theories

The Renaissance was also an age of prophecies and astrologers, and not all scholars and scientists were immune to their influence. Some who studied fossils invoked the influence of the stars, and others speculated about mysterious natural forces with strange properties.

Fossils, they argued, were anything but organic in
origin – a far cry from the view that had been held by a
number of ancient Greeks. According to one Renaissance
theory, fossils were formed from tiny stone seeds that
grew and then perished inside the earth. Another
speculator held that they were 'trial runs' the Creator
had decided not to infuse with life. Backing up his theory
with numerous illustrations, he asserted that 'Nature
learned to make the human body' by producing fossils
shaped like human organs.

According to still another school of thought, Satan had
created fossils in a vain attempt to emulate God. For that
matter, why couldn't they simply be curious 'sports of
nature' attributable solely to chance? In 1565 Conrad
Gesner described the distinctive shapes mineral

substances – including fossils, which he called 'figure stones' – could assume in *De Omni Rerum Fossilium Lapidum et Gemmarum Figuris et Similitudinibis Liber* (A Book on Fossil Objects, Chiefly Stones and Gems, Their Shapes and Appearance), a superbly illustrated compendium of all major fossils known at the time.

A few enlightened souls in the Middle Ages opt for a more rational approach

The Greek thinkers had not fallen into total oblivion. Their manuscripts, translated and relayed by Arab philosophers, had found their way to the West. Around the year 1000, Persian philosopher Ibn Sīnā (also known as Avicenna) hinted at the true nature of fossils in his *Book of the Remedy.*

In the 13th century, Albertus Magnus, a Dominican scholastic philosopher (and, briefly, bishop of Regensburg) who studied Avicenna and occasionally took issue with classical authors, echoed this interpretation. At about the same time, Roger Bacon, an English Franciscan monk, advocated research, experimentation and the creation of a new science freed from the burden of the ancients. For his efforts he spent fourteen years in prison on suspicion of heresy. Also at this time, other scholars were beginning to advance theories to account for the formation of mountains and layers of sediment.

In the 16th century, Leonardo da Vinci's wide-ranging interests included, not surprisingly, fossils, whose origins he correctly explained. His categorical rejection of spontaneous generation made him a pioneer in stratigraphy, the study of the origin, composition, distribution and succession of the earth's layers.

A half-century later, in France, an 'unlettered potter' named Bernard Palissy (1510–89) collected and studied petrified shells and fish. 'I have drawn a number of pictures of the petrified shells that can be found by the thousands in the Ardennes Mountains, and not just shells, but fish .... I have found more kinds of petrified fish, or the shells thereof, than I have of modern kinds now living in the sea.' About 1580 the academics at the Sorbonne, part of the

This fossil sea lily stalk was labelled *petra stellaris,* or 'star stone' in Conrad Gesner's work (illustration below and title page opposite above).

Bernard Palissy argued that 'before the said seashells were petrified, the fish that formed them were alive therein'. His lectures were attended by physicians, surgeons, mathematicians and throngs of curious onlookers (drawing opposite below).

University of Paris, transfixed with indignation, listened as he refuted spontaneous generation and asserted that fossils were not sports of nature but the remains of living things. Imprisoned for his religious views, Palissy died in the Bastille prison, an unsung genius.

Shells and fish are among the first fossils to be correctly identified

Conrad Gesner, who coined the word 'figure stone', had noted the similarity between *glossopetrae* and shark teeth. In a treatise published in 1616, geologist Fabio Colonna (1567–1650) showed that these remains were indeed shark teeth and were often found together with marine mollusc shells, which he also believed to be the remains of living things.

It took many years finally to establish the connection between *glossopetrae* (opposite below) and the forbidding jaws of sharks (left). But even correct identification could not completely divest 'tongue stones' of their magical aura. In the late 17th century the German philosopher Leibniz acknowledged that their curative powers had been exaggerated, and then recommended them as a tooth cleanser!

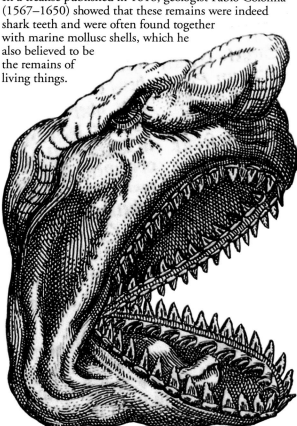

Some fifty years later, Niels Stensen (1638–86), a Dane who studied anatomy in Copenhagen and France and was acclaimed for his expert dissections, corroborated this diagnosis after examining the head of a large shark that had been recently brought ashore from the Mediterranean. If Stensen was aware of Colonna's earlier research, he made no mention of it. 'Tongue stones' did not grow within rocks, he argued, but were buried in a kind of mud. The earth's surface had risen, and that was why they were found high above sea level.

In 1665, Stensen (left) moved to Florence at the invitation of Grand Duke Ferdinand II de' Medici, whose support allowed him to conduct anatomical research in one of the city's hospitals. At the behest of the grand duke, a shark's head was brought to Stensen for dissection, which led to the correct identification of 'tongue stones.'

Because sharks are cartilaginous fish, the discovery of even fragments of fossil shark skeletons was a rare occurrence. Shark teeth, however, were found in abundance.

Stensen sets forth a fundamental law of stratigraphy: younger sediments always form on top of older ones

Fossil finds could now be investigated according to a relatively logical time scale. An unbreakable link between the history of fossils and geology had been forged.

A Protestant who, in 1667, had converted to Catholicism after moving to Italy, Stensen gave up his scientific pursuits at the age of forty and entered the priesthood, perhaps because he found it difficult to reconcile his scientific discoveries with his religious beliefs.

His theories sparked heated debate among intellectuals, especially since he had corresponded regularly with naturalists outside Italy, in particular, the fellows of the Royal Society in London.

Giants and surgeons

One day in January 1613, some workers found a number of huge bones and a tooth while digging in a sandpit outside Romans, a town in southeastern France. The local landowner, Marquis Nicolas de Langon, consulted experts from the University of Montpellier. They decided that these were giant humans' bones. The ruling was corroborated by the scholars' counterparts at Grenoble, but some academicians voiced doubts and maintained that they were the remains of a huge animal, possibly an elephant, a rhinoceros or a whale. Fuelled periodically by vituperative personal attacks, a fierce debate raged for several years and often degenerated into reprisals between factions of barber-surgeons, physicians and anatomists. 'Pro-giant' surgeon and anatomist Nicolas Habicot came out with *Gigantostéologie ou Discours des Os d'un Géant* (Gigantosteology, or Discourse on the Bones of a Giant); a Professor Riolan, an anatomist and botanist, countered with *Gigantomachie pour Répondre à la Gigantostéologie* (Gigantomachy, in Reply to Gigantosteology), slipping in cutting remarks about the surgeons' guild.

GIGANTOLOGIE

HISTOIRE
DE LA GRANDEVR
DES GEANTS,

Où il est demonstré, que toute
ancienneté les plus grands hom-
mes, & Geants, n'ont esté plus
hauts que ceux de ce
temps.

*Quis autem vestrum assiduè cogitans po-
test adjicere ad staturam suam cubi-
tum unum?* Matthei cap. 6.

A PARIS,
Chez ADRIAN PERIER, ruë Sainct
Iacques,
M. DC. XVIII.

The battle of tracts and pamphlets dragged on until 1618. What became of the bones is uncertain, but in 1984 the tooth was identified as belonging to a *Deinotherium giganteum*, a type of early elephant.

The acrimony of this debate shows that in the early 17th century – and for some time to come – people clung to legends even as progress was being made by those intent on finding a rational explanation for large vertebrate remains.

After obtaining some gigantic bones from the Marquis de Langon, Pierre Mazurier, a barber-surgeon by profession, travelled from town to town, satisfying the public's appetite for blood-curdling yarns by exhibiting them (for a fee) as the remains of Theutobochus, king of the Teutons, the Cimbri and the Ambrones. (These Germanic tribes had, in fact, struck terror into the hearts of Europeans nearly two years earlier.) Could a man who – before meeting defeat at the hands of the Roman consul Marius – led an army four hundred strong on a devastating rampage through Gaul and the Iberian peninsula have been anything but a giant? To back up his assertions, Mazurier claimed – without ever actually producing it – that a stone bearing an inscription of the giant's name in Latin had been found with bones 7.5 metres long and a tooth weighing some 5 kilos. A number of Mazurier's bones were later removed to Fontainebleau and temporarily displayed in the private quarters of the queen mother, Marie de Médicis.

Title page (left) of a 17th-century French treatise on giants.

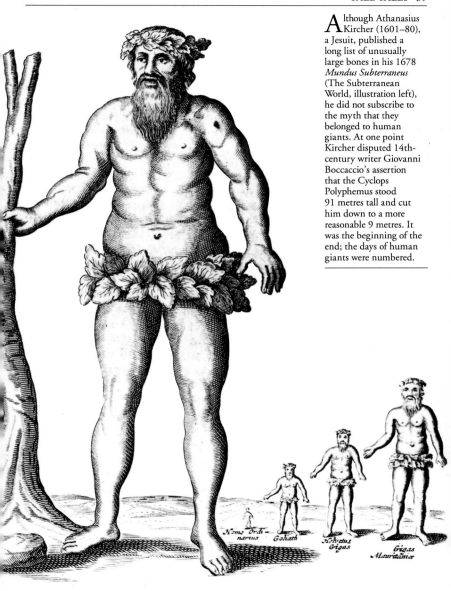

Although Athanasius Kircher (1601–80), a Jesuit, published a long list of unusually large bones in his 1678 *Mundus Subterraneus* (The Subterranean World, illustration left), he did not subscribe to the myth that they belonged to human giants. At one point Kircher disputed 14th-century writer Giovanni Boccaccio's assertion that the Cyclops Polyphemus stood 91 metres tall and cut him down to a more reasonable 9 metres. It was the beginning of the end; the days of human giants were numbered.

Tab.I.a.

Georg Wolfg. Knorr exc.

B.VI

The wonders of nature…

Georg Wolfgang Knorr (1705–61) and Johann Emmanuel Walch's (1724–78) four-volume *Sammlung der Merkwürdigkeiten der Natur, und Altertümer des Erdbodens, Welche Petrificierte Körper Enthält* (Collection of Wonders of Nature and Antiquities of the Earth, Comprising Petrified Bodies) was published in Nuremberg, Germany, between 1755 and 1778. Walch wrote the bulk of the text; the magnificent colour plates (opposite, ammonites; left, gastropods) were personally engraved by Knorr, who was both an artist and a natural scientist. Knorr and Walch ventured to speculate about the duration of the 'catastrophes' that, according to their estimates, had convulsed the surface of the earth several thousand years earlier. Fossils, they concluded, did not all date from the same period and could therefore be traced back to more than one causative event – an intriguing hypothesis at the time.

hn. J.E.J.Walchii, Eloquent.& Poes.Prof.publ.in Acad.Ienensi

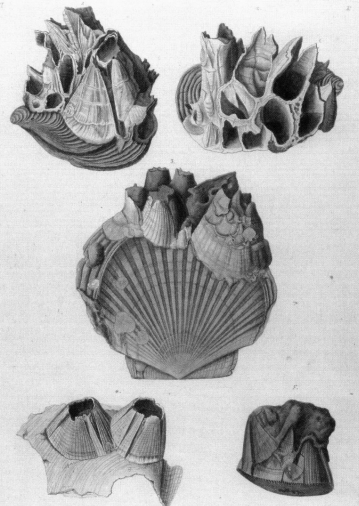

Ex Mußæo D. Joh: Jac: d'Amone Ph: et J. V. D. Basileens.

43

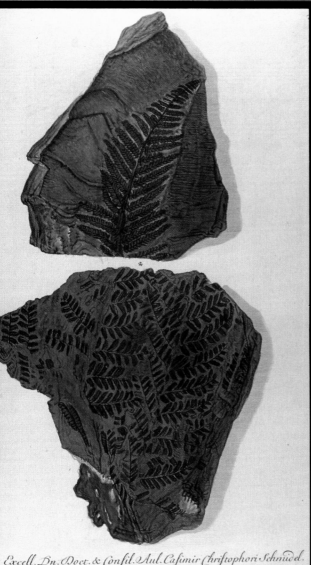

Excell. Dn. Doct. & Confil. Aul. Cafimir Chriftophori Schmidel.

158.

... and antiquities of the Earth

In their essentially descriptive book, Knorr and Walch concentrated on fossil shells and invertebrates but did not overlook plants and assorted 'petrifactions'. However, skeletal remains of vertebrates – or, as they were called at the time, 'osteoliths' – were under-represented because the authors considered them less interesting. One engraving (opposite) shows shells and crustaceans, including barnacles; another (left), fossilized impressions of ferns.

As anatomists make headway, the giants gradually lose ground

Dissections and descriptions of living animals by the likes of Edward Tyson (1650–1708) in England and Claude Perrault (1613–88) in France shed new light on the osteology of many vertebrates (that is, the structure and organization of their bones). Comparisons of these bones with fossil counterparts from quarries showed that the latter belonged to animals, not human giants. In 1688, Campani, an anatomist based in Rome, compared fossil bones found at Vitorchiano (Italy) with casts of an elephant skeleton from the Medici family's collection in Florence. He deduced from their striking similarities that the gigantic bones from Italy belonged to an elephant-like animal. At long last, the Cyclops of Mount Etna had been correctly identified.

Where did they come from? Where did they go?

The theory that fossils were once living things gradually gained acceptance in intellectual circles. But new questions cropped up. How did elephants, those denizens of tropical climates, come to die in temperate zones? How did they get there? And why did certain fossils, such as ammonites and belemnites, lack equivalents in modern nature?

What fate had befallen these huge animals whose remains were now being discovered in ever greater numbers? Could they possibly be species that no longer existed? Unthinkable! That would imply that the Creation had been less than perfect, that God had allowed a part of his Creation to die out. Clearly, such a conclusion would have been diametrically opposed to prevailing Christian doctrine. Only a few thinkers, such as the great British scientist Robert Hooke (1635-1703), were beginning to question received ideas.

In an early attempt to reconstruct animals from fossil remains, German physicist Otto von Guericke (1602–86) pieced together some mammoth (and probably rhinoceros) bones that had been discovered in Germany in 1663. The result was a fantastic creature with no hind legs and a horn 'five ells long' in the middle of its forehead. Guericke's drawing of this composite comes from Leibniz's *Protogaea* (1749).

The mighty waters of the Flood had transported them from their native land to their present location

Though hardly a new concept, this was the consensus of opinion by the 18th century. As far back as the late 13th century, Ristoro d'Arezzo, an Italian monk, suggested that shells found in mountains had been transported there by the Flood. In their day, Leonardo da Vinci and Bernard Palissy disputed this line of reasoning. Nevertheless, it attracted a good many proponents and by the 18th century had burgeoned into a school of thought known as diluvialism. With German philosopher Gottfried Wilhelm Leibniz (1646–1716) as their standard-bearer, a number of philosophers subscribed to this hypothesis because it made the organic origin of fossils more acceptable. Surely, they reasoned, the vanished descendants of the fossil

❛ The flood was forty days upon the earth; ... And the waters prevailed exceedingly upon the earth; and all the high hills, that were under the whole heaven, were covered. Fifteen cubits upward did the waters prevail; and the mountains were covered. And all flesh died that moved upon the earth, both of fowl, and of cattle, and of beast, and of every creeping thing that creepeth upon the earth, and every man. ❜
Genesis 7:17–21

animals would turn up one day in lands still unexplored. The assumption was that the living counterparts of fossil marine organisms, such as ammonites, awaited discovery somewhere in the ocean depths. This led to wide-ranging speculation about the history of the earth and about the Flood itself.

How fossils came to be regarded as proof positive of the veracity of Scripture

Swiss naturalist Johann Jakob Scheuchzer, a pioneering palaeontologist in his day, was one of the most ardent supporters of the Flood theory. Adopting a lighthearted approach, he defended his views in *Piscium Querelae et Vindiciae* (Complaints and Claims of the Fishes), an illustrated pamphlet in which fossil fishes voice 'complaints and claims' about their being innocent victims of a flood brought on by the sins of humankind – the very race now bent on contesting their status as once-living creatures and degrading them to mere inorganic formations. And what about the antediluvian (pre-Flood) sinners? When two vertebrae were unearthed at the university town of Altdorf (Switzerland), Scheuchzer first claimed that the bones were their remains. They were human vertebrae, to be sure, but not as old as the naturalist so readily assumed them to be. Nevertheless, the scarcity of human fossils troubled him.

Then in 1725 Scheuchzer triumphantly produced what he claimed to be a skeleton of *Homo diluvii testis,* an ill-fated 'man, a witness of the Flood and who had seen God',

Author of numerous books on fossil plants and animals and passionate defender of their organic origin, Scheuchzer (left) was instrumental in disseminating information about fossils. He kept up a voluminous correspondence with contemporary scientists, including Leibniz and English physicist John Woodward, both of whom were staunch diluvialists. Engravings of fossils, which Scheuchzer regarded as innocent victims of the Flood, grace his *Physica Sacra* (Sacred Physics), 1731, a quasiscientific commentary on the Bible.

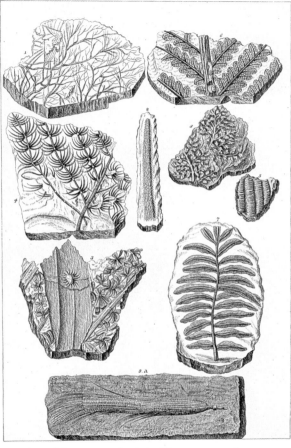

Fossil plants figured prominently in speculation about the Flood, and Scheuchzer's *Herbarium Diluvianum* (Herbarium of the Deluge), 1709, was one of the first books to deal specifically with the subject. Numerous drawings of Carboniferous floras, chiefly ferns (left), attest to his attention to detail and commitment to accuracy. The featured specimens range from insects, madrepores and ammonites (including details of serrated chambers) to simple dendrites and 'natural monstrosities' generated by nothing but an overactive imagination.

a vestige of the accursed original human race that had been swallowed up by the universal deluge. Here was both tangible proof that the Flood had actually taken place and a cautionary tale for sinners. It was not identified, more accurately, as a 'petrified lizard' until 1787; in 1825 French naturalist Georges Cuvier (1769–1832) proclaimed the skeleton to be 'an unknown species of giant aquatic salamander'.

Kolm

Auf der Werch

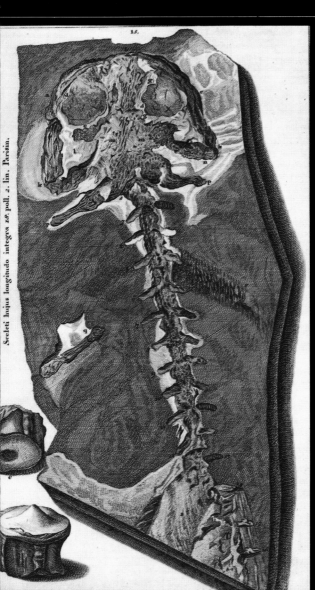

Sceleti hujus longitudo integra 20. poll. 2. lin. Parisin.

15.

'A witness of the Flood'

In 1725 a peculiar fossil skeleton 1.20 metres long was discovered in Miocene (7- to 26-million-year-old) sediment at the Ohningen quarry, near Lake Constance in Europe. When consulted about the specimen, Scheuchzer confidently identified the remains as those of 'a Man, Witness of the Flood' and christened it *Homo diluvii testis*. In a detailed, illustrated description of the fossil (1731), he concluded that 'the reality of the Universal Deluge, albeit acknowledged for many centuries, has never been more patent than it is at the present time'. Later correctly identified as a giant salamander, the fossil 'man' is now in the Teyler Museum in Haarlem, in the Netherlands, where it was named Andrias Scheuchzer.

The illustrations here and overleaf are from Scheuchzer's *Herbarium Diluvianum*.

The Creation

⁶The earth was without form, and void; and darkness was upon the face of the deep. And the Spirit of God moved upon the face of the waters. And God said, Let there be light: and there was light. And God saw the light, that it was good: and God divided the light from the darkness. And God called the light Day, and the darkness he called Night.... And God said, Let the waters under the heaven be gathered together unto one place, and let the dry land appear.... And God said, Let the earth bring forth grass...; and it was so.... And God said, Let the waters bring forth abundantly the moving creature that hath life, and fowl that may fly above the earth in the open firmament of heaven.... And God said, Let the earth bring forth the living creature after his kind, cattle, and creeping thing, and beast of the earth after his kind: and it was so.... And God said, Let us make man in our image, after our likeness.... And it was so.⁹

Genesis 1:2–30

How old could they be?

This and other attempts to determine the age of fossils led to speculation about the age of the earth. According to the book of Genesis, the whole of Creation – heaven, earth, sea, plants, animals and humans – had lasted six days. On the sixth day 'God created man'. That was enough for the Middle Ages. In 1650 James Ussher (1581–1656), archbishop of Armagh, Ireland, concluded from his scholarly analysis of the Bible that the Creation had taken place on 26 October 4004 BC – a finding the religious community at the time considered sound. Scheuchzer ventured another estimate: the Flood (hence, the 'death' of fossils) occurred two hundred and fifty years before the building of the Great Pyramid at Giza in Egypt.

Naturalist Louis Bourguet went even farther back in time. In 1729, after examining layers of sediment, he announced that sixteen centuries had elapsed between the Creation and the Flood. We ought not to make light of these estimates: for a branch of science that was still in its infancy, sixteen centuries was a virtually inconceivable period of time. In any event, the Bible, which went largely if not totally unchallenged, had set the earth's history in a strict chronological time frame that kept overzealous theorists at bay.

In 1766 a huge animal skull, its jaws studded with forbidding teeth, was unearthed on Pietersberg (St Peter's Mountain), near Maastricht (the Netherlands) and promptly became the focal point of a bitter tug-of-war. Church authorities ordered Dr Hoffmann, a former German army surgeon and noted fossil collector who had supervised its excavation, to turn the specimen over to Canon Godin, who held title to the ground. Above: a 1799 engraving of the discovery.

Misgivings arise

While at the end of the 18th century the ocean depths were as mysterious as ever, uncharted lands – the presumed last refuges of animals that apparently had vanished from the known world – had become increasingly scarce. Some naturalists were starting to conclude that the majority of large vertebrates had been identified. The Flood might account for the death of individual animals and their disappearance

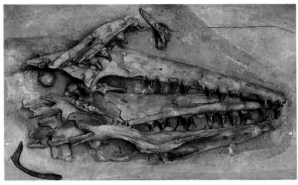

from a particular region (such as Europe's vanished elephants), but not the extinction of an entire species. All kinds of hypotheses now surfaced: cataclysmic inundations ('catastrophes', as they

In 1795 Godin hid the fossil from French geologist Barthélemy Faujas de Saint-Fond, who, during this time of political unrest, wished to transport it to France for further study. Six hundred bottles of wine were promised to anyone who could determine its whereabouts. The specimen was duly found and sent back to Paris. Scientists puzzled over the creature. Was it a cetacean? No, a crocodile, argued Hoffmann and Faujas. 'Prior to the period of upheaval and submersion that entombed these amphibians and indiscriminately threw them together with shellfish,' wrote Faujas, 'they lived in a far earlier age, breeding in the rivers and lakes which, if animals of this kind were to flourish, must at one time have existed amid great land masses.'

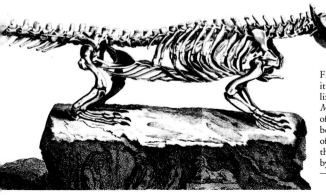

Finally Cuvier identified it as a gigantic marine lizard and named it *Mosasaurus,* the 'reptile of the Meuse'. Left below: an engraving of a reconstruction of the skeleton in a treatise by Faujas.

were called in the 19th century); changes in the earth's climate (to account for the finding in Europe of fossil remains of animals living in tropical regions); extermination by humans; the temporary introduction by humans of species that were unable to adapt; and the remains of pagan sacrifices. Tongue firmly in cheek, the eminent French philosopher Voltaire (1694–1778) contended that seashells found on mountaintops had been left there by pilgrims on their way to Santiago de Compostela, a pilgrimage site in northwestern Spain.

Georges-Louis Leclerc de Buffon (1707–88) is the first to suspect how far back the history of the Earth really went

According to Buffon's calculations, Adam and Eve came into being 6000 to 8000 years before him; the earth, however, he believed had been in existence for 75,000 years.

Buffon's estimate was, of course, far from accurate; but no one before him had ventured figures of this magnitude. He divided the history of the earth into six epochs and argued that various life-forms had appeared as conditions gradually allowed. Then came the seventh epoch during which 'the power of Man was added to that of Nature'. Although Buffon did not refute the Flood theory outright, he felt that the event actually had had little impact on the history of the world. The changes that occurred on the earth's surface had resulted instead from the action of the sea and the erosive effect of flowing water.

Fossils, Buffon asserted, witnessed the earliest periods in the planet's history. These once-living things had

HISTOIRE
NATURELLE,
GÉNÉRALE ET PARTICULIÈRE.
AVEC LA DESCRIPTION
DU CABINET DU ROI.

Tome Premier.

A PARIS,
DE L'IMPRIMERIE ROYALE.
M. DCCXLIX.

The dynamic and industrious Buffon (opposite) studied law, medicine, geology and mathematics, devoted much time to botany, and travelled throughout France, Italy and England. He owned a foundry and proved a shrewd businessman. In 1739 a friend of his, the minister Maurepas, secured for Buffon the directorship of what is now Paris's Museum of Natural History, into which position Buffon then channelled all his energy. He expanded the garden grounds, added new specimens and turned the museum into one of the leading institutions of its kind. The forty-four volumes of his *Histoire Naturelle* (title page, left) were published between 1749 and 1789; the entire run of the first three volumes (one thousand copies, in 1749) sold out in six weeks. Buffon's *Histoire Naturelle* was one of the most widely read books of the 18th century. He published his pioneering ideas about the history of our planet in 1771 in *Les Epoques de la nature* (The Epochs of Nature).

actually inhabited the places where their remains were found – proof that cold regions were warm at one time. The constitution of animals could not have so changed, to quote Buffon, as to 'give the elephant the disposition of the reindeer'. The presence of large fossil mammals in many northern countries suggested to him that present-day Europe, Asia and North America long ago comprised a single land mass.

Buffon went on to say that some animal groups existed solely as fossils and had no living counterparts; the species that died out had, he suspected, adapted the least well.

The theologians of the Sorbonne took a dim view of Buffon's audacity, notwithstanding his protestations of

In the early 18th century, a system for classifying plants and animals had not yet been devised. Increasingly diverse specimens from all over the world were thrown together indiscriminately in natural history collections. Fossils were often compared with present-day organisms, but criteria were loosely defined at best. In *Systema Naturae* (1735), Linnaeus (left) introduced the concept of binomial nomenclature, which provided all scientific disciplines with an essential classifying tool still in use today. Human knowledge was expanding, and with it the commitment to standardize all fields of inquiry.

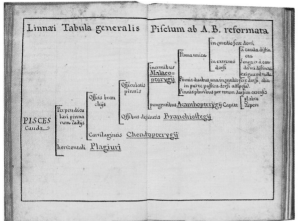

Linnæi Tabula generalis   Piscium ab A. B. reformata

PISCES
Cauda

horizontali Plagiuri

Perpendiculari pinnarum cædijs

Cartilagineis Chondopterygij

Ossibus dejantis Branchioltegij

Ossis branchijs

Officulatis pinnis

Incrmibus Malaco= pterygij

Pinnis duabus una in medio fere dorsi, alia in parte postica dorsi adiposa.

Pinnis pluribus per rotum dorsum extensis

pungnibus Acanthopterygij Capite

glabro
aspero

Pinna unica

in media fere dorsi

in extremo dorsi

à cauda distincta

à cauda distincta

exigua vel nulla

L innaeus described tens of thousands of individual plants and animals and assigned a two-part Latin name to each of them. Now each and every life-form could be identified by its genus and particular species. For example, the toucan (genus Ramphastos) comprises thirty-seven species, among them *Ramphastos cuvieri* (literally, Cuvier's toucan). Systematic classification could also be applied to extinct life-forms, which were likewise sorted by genus and species. Above left: a diagram in *Systema Naturae*.

innocence and claims that his intention had been to reconcile the natural sciences with theology. But Buffon enjoyed the protection of the French king and was spared official Church censure. Acclaimed for their elegance and readability, Buffon's writings were profoundly influential and earned him a place in history as a pioneer in the popularization of science.

Meanwhile, Swedish botanist Carl von Linné (also known as Linnaeus, 1707–78) refines the notions of genus and species and makes them the building blocks of binomial nomenclature

Under the system devised by Linnaeus each individual form that ever lived was (and still is) assigned a genus name followed by a species name: roughly the equivalent of a person's last name and first name. The criteria Linnaeus selected for his systematic arrangement could be applied to all organisms without exception, animals and plants alike, past or present. Now fossils could take their place in a general classification of natural phenomena.

Paris, January 1796. A young man was about to read a paper before the distinguished fellows of the French National Institute of Arts and Sciences. His name: Georges Cuvier. A native of Montbéliard, a town in eastern France, he had been in Paris for barely six months, but his audience knew that this twenty-six-year-old naturalist already had a lifetime of experience behind him.

CHAPTER 3
THE AGE OF SCIENTISTS

❛ I am gathering material for some great future anatomist, and when that person comes along, I should like to be credited with having paved the way.❜
Georges Cuvier

A 19th-century painting of a pterodactyl (opposite).

As a boy, Cuvier filled his notebooks with sketches of the animals he had read about in Buffon. When he finished secondary school – at the age of fifteen – the Duke of Württemberg (whose domain then included Cuvier's home town) offered him a scholarship to attend an academy in Stuttgart. Accepting this token of esteem, Cuvier decided on the 'philosophy' department, which really meant he would receive a scientifically oriented education. Upon graduation four years later, the next logical step would have been the German civil service; instead, with his father's help, the nineteen-year-old was hired as a tutor for a wealthy Protestant family in the Caux region of Normandy. This was to prove a fortuitous opportunity. Cuvier spent his spare time collecting fish and molluscs. He dissected, described and, most importantly, compared specimens, recording his observations in a series of notebooks, the *Diarium Zoologicum.*

Meanwhile, Paris rumbled with unrest, the Bastille fell, the people of France rose up in revolution, the aristocrats emigrated, the king plotted and fled – only to find himself arrested and guillotined – and the Republic was proclaimed.

Far removed though Cuvier was from the events of the French Revolution, they were to work in his favour. Abbé Tessier, a noted agronomist and, when in Paris, a welcome visitor at the Museum of Natural History, returned in 1793 to his native Caux. There he was introduced to Cuvier and, impressed by the young man's notebooks, he immediately brought them to the attention of his friends at the museum in Paris. Soon afterwards, a new species of ray was named after Cuvier in honour of its discoverer.

In 1795 Cuvier received a note from Etienne Geoffroy Saint-Hilaire, a teacher of zoology at the Museum of Natural History and founder of the zoo affiliated with the museum: 'Come to Paris and take your place as a second Linnaeus, a new lawgiver in natural history.'

Cuvier described and drew the animals he observed (left, a salamander, and opposite, a bird) in his notebooks, the *Diarium Zoologicum.*

An 1813 view (below) of the Jardin du Roi (Museum of Natural History) in Paris.

Cuvier arrived in the capital that summer and soon found himself teaching animal anatomy at the museum. In 1802 he was appointed professor of comparative anatomy, a position he held for the rest of his life.

But let us return to the lecture.

Cuvier sets forth the fundamental laws of comparative anatomy: subordination and correlation of organs

What Cuvier would say that day he had deduced from his research on living animals back in Normandy. He had done more than just examine each of the specimens he had collected. By progressing to the more instructive stage of comparative analysis, he was able to show that certain vital

❛ The nation of [17]92, which moved along at breakneck speed, saved the Jardin du Roi on a whim. Some cultivated individuals banded together and persuaded the French people that the Royal Garden was a great repository of medicinal herbs where the sick might come in search of bodily well-being.... They also pointed out that the chemistry laboratory might be useful in the production of gunpowder. For these reasons, the Royal Garden was spared.... A directive was issued whereby the Royal Garden would henceforth be known as the Museum of Natural History.❜

M. Boitard
Le Jardin des Plantes, 1842

Young Cuvier taught natural history (left, lecturing at the Sorbonne) before he was offered the chair of animal anatomy at the Museum of Natural History as soon as it became vacant in 1802. From then on, the position was known as the chair of comparative anatomy.

Cuvier's drawing of a mammoth skeleton (below).

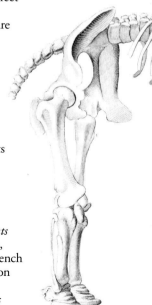

organs are organized in such a way as inevitably to affect other organs (law of subordination) and that some anatomical features are interdependent while others are mutually exclusive (law of correlation).

He set forth his conclusions in *Discours sur les Révolutions de la Surface du Globe* (Discourse on the Revolutions of the Surface of the Globe), first published in 1825: 'Every organism constitutes a whole, a unique and self-contained system, the constituent parts of which are interactive and which, through reciprocal response, conspire to bring about one and the same ultimate action. None of these parts can change without causing the others to change; consequently, each one, individually considered, provides the key to all the others.'

Studying fossils leads Cuvier to palaeontology

In his reading of his *Mémoire sur les Espèces d'Eléphants tant Vivants que Fossiles* (Treatise on Elephant Species, Both Living and Fossils) before the meeting of the French Institute, Cuvier gave a detailed anatomical description of bones from Europe, Siberia, North and South America, Africa and India. He also identified *Elephas primigenius,* or the Russian mammoth. Elephants, he concluded, were in fact indigenous to the regions where their fossil remains were found. They had not been brought there by humans (as some had argued, citing Hannibal leading elephants across the Alps and other examples from classical antiquity). Their demise had resulted instead from a change in the earth's climate; but the change was sudden, not gradual. Cuvier did not venture to say the exact cause, stating only that their burial had resulted from a 'general inundation' and letting the matter rest there.

Cuvier's work from this period, and much of what was to follow, was collected and published in 1812 as *Recherches sur les Ossements Fossiles des Quadrupèdes* (Researches on the Fossil Bones of Quadrupeds), which Cuvier revised and expanded as time went on.

Cuvier drew a salamander (above) in his *Diarium Zoologicum* during a visit to the British Museum.

Cuvier is determined to mobilize as much research material as he can

The Museum of Natural History in Paris was a repository of countless fossils of every description, and Cuvier started wading through its collections as soon as he arrived. But other material lay deep inside the hills of nearby Montmartre and Ménilmontant, quarried since Roman times for gypsum, used in making plaster of Paris. A useful building stone, gypsum also preserves organic remains.

Many came to hear him lecture. He had a following of eager young people, medical students for the most part, intent on learning what they could from him about anatomy. Between classes he would dissect specimens, the way he used to in Normandy, and mounted them so that they might be preserved.
Professor Louis Roule,
Cuvier: Historien Scientifique, 1932

For a fee, a quarrier by the name of Varin brought Cuvier everything he found.

Intent on examining all the vertebrate fossils he could get his hands on, Cuvier hunted down specimens and data all over Europe. He visited storerooms in which intellectuals and amateur scientists of centuries past had garnered their treasures. A day did not go by that fossil remains did not turn up somewhere; there were data and descriptions to be obtained. He circulated a letter requesting information from natural scientists all over the world.

The laws of comparative anatomy make it possible to reconstruct vanished species from as little as a single tooth

It followed from Cuvier's methodology that if one had a vital piece of an animal's anatomy, the teeth in particular, the remaining components would fall into place. 'If the intestines of an animal are so organized as to digest freshly obtained flesh, then its jaws must be constructed to devour prey, its claws to grasp and tear it apart,

❛ I cannot fail to marvel at this trove of fossil animal remains ... that nature concentrated in the quarries surrounding our city as if she had laid them by for the edification of the present age.❜
Georges Cuvier

its teeth to cut and divide it, the whole structure of its organs of motion to pursue and overtake it, and its sensory organs to detect it at a distance; nature must even have placed in its brain the necessary instinct so that it would know how to stalk and ambush its victims.'

Then came a wonderful opportunity to demonstrate his technique. One day, while digging in the Montmartre gypsum quarries, Cuvier came across a small jawbone with teeth he felt sure belonged to an opossum, a small marsupial now found only in Australia and the Americas. Based solely on the character and development of the animal's teeth, he predicted that he would find the characteristic pouch bones of marsupials once the rest of the skeleton was removed from its matrix (the stone in which it was

Cuvier's drawing (opposite) of a mastodon tooth.

In the 18th century, the region of Paris known as Montmartre (shown here in an 1850 lithograph) still lay outside the city limits. Quarries and limekilns once dotted the hillside, and a number of fossils turned up at the site as far back as 1783. Cuvier (below) initiated systematic excavations on Montmartre and discovered the remains of now-extinct herbivores and carnivores, including the celebrated 'Montmartre opossum'.

embedded). The event was carefully staged in front of a number of Cuvier's colleagues. His prediction came true before their very eyes. Cuvier tried to put into words what he felt when faced with the daunting task of reconstruction. 'I was in the position of a man who had been given pell-mell the mutilated, fragmentary remains of several hundred skeletons belonging to twenty kinds of animals. Each bone had to be reunited with its appropriate mate; it was a virtual resurrection, and there was no all-powerful trumpet at my command. But the immutable laws prescribed to living things served in its stead; and when comparative anatomy spoke, every bone, every scrap of bone, fell into place. I cannot describe the pleasure this afforded me.'

'[He] has reconstructed entire worlds from a few bleached bones.... He has quickened the dead'

Interest in Cuvier's discoveries surged among his contemporaries; his work even made its presence felt

❧ The fossil remains of an animal [the opossum], a genus now confined exclusively to America, lie within our quarries.... The features imprinted therein are so faint that they cannot be made out except on very close inspection; and yet, how precious those features are! They are the imprint of an animal of which there is no other surviving trace.... The animal was trapped in a fairly lifelike position.❧

Georges Cuvier

Cuvier's drawings of the 'Montmartre opossum' (below).

in the literature of the day. Novelist Honoré de Balzac paid tribute to him in a lyrical passage in *La Peau de Chagrin* (1831):

Have you ever been plunged into the immensity of space and time while reading Cuvier's books on geology? Our immortal naturalist has reconstructed entire worlds from a few bleached bones; like Cadmus, rebuilt cities with teeth; restored all the mysteries of zoology to countless forests from a few pieces of coal; and rediscovered entire populations of giants from the footprint of a mammoth. He has quickened the dead.... Suddenly, marble takes on an animal shape, death is infused with life, the history of the world unfolds before you.

Cuvier's laws of comparative anatomy gained widespread acceptance among scientists, even those who were sharply divided over his views on the history of the earth.

• No question but that there were...two saurian species that flew by means of a wing-membrane attached to a single finger of their hands; that used the other three fingers...to keep themselves aloft...; that stood only on their hind legs and had large heads and huge gaping mouths bristling with small, sharp teeth suitable only for catching insects and small animals.**•** This is how Cuvier described the pterodactyl, a flying reptile he had identified based on a skeleton from Bavaria (reconstruction of 1941 above by Burian).

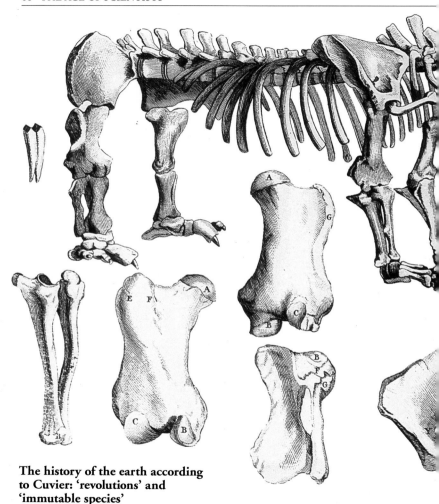

The history of the earth according to Cuvier: 'revolutions' and 'immutable species'

Working with fossils involved Cuvier more deeply in geology; he had somehow to determine the chronological sequence of the life-forms he was resurrecting. With the help of Alexandre Brongniart (1770–1847), a young geologist, he studied the fossil-rich formations of the

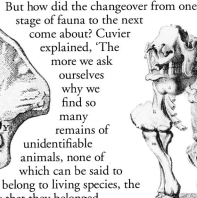

Paris basin. Four years of measuring, recording data and comparison culminated in 1811 in the jointly written *Essai sur la Géographie Minéralogique des Environs de Paris* (Essay on the Mineral Geography of the Paris Region), which featured a coloured map of seven geological strata together with their corresponding lithological characteristics and fossils. The fossils enabled them to work out a time scale and delineate a number of different stages in the earth's history.

Diverse faunas, Cuvier argued, had come into being successively, each replacing the one that had lived and died out before it. But how did the changeover from one stage of fauna to the next come about? Cuvier explained, 'The more we ask ourselves why we find so many remains of unidentifiable animals, none of which can be said to belong to living species, the likelier it seems that they belonged to creatures wiped out by some revolution of the globe, creatures that have since been replaced by those living today.' His choice of words mirrored the times. Just as

In 1788 a gigantic skeleton the size of an elephant was found near Buenos Aires, Argentina, and ceremoniously delivered to Charles III of Spain. Dubbed the 'animal from Paraguay,' it was mounted at once and displayed in a presumably lifelike position. Drawings of the specimen circulated throughout Europe and found their way to Cuvier. He named it *Megatherium americanum* and, struck by its similarity to the sloth, classified it in the same order.

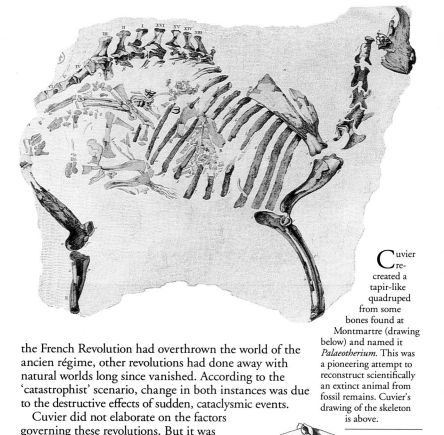

Cuvier re-created a tapir-like quadruped from some bones found at Montmartre (drawing below) and named it *Palaeotherium*. This was a pioneering attempt to reconstruct scientifically an extinct animal from fossil remains. Cuvier's drawing of the skeleton is above.

the French Revolution had overthrown the world of the ancien régime, other revolutions had done away with natural worlds long since vanished. According to the 'catastrophist' scenario, change in both instances was due to the destructive effects of sudden, cataclysmic events.

Cuvier did not elaborate on the factors governing these revolutions. But it was obvious, to him at least, that living things did not evolve. The mummified animals, particularly the ibises, that Napoleon's campaigns had brought back from Egypt were proof enough for him: the five-thousand-year-old carcasses were identical to living ibises in every detail. They had undergone no changes; no transformation had taken place. Species were immutable, fixed. In Cuvier's day, five thousand years was considered a very long time – sufficiently long, he contended, for species transformation, had there been any. Besides, if such transformations had occurred, intermediate forms would have come to light. Such was not the case. Later, other scientists were to show that these particular aspects of Cuvier's hypothesis were flawed.

Jean-Baptiste de Monet de Lamarck (1744–1829) counters Cuvier's immutability with transformation of species

A physician and botanist by training, Lamarck was appointed professor of zoology at the Museum of Natural History in 1793. He went on to specialize in invertebrates and worked out a systematic arrangement of species, parts of which are still considered valid today. While examining the Tertiary (from 2- to 65-million-year-old) shells of the Paris region in particular, he noted that some species still existed exactly as they had been, pointing to continuity of life, and that other species had been slightly modified, suggesting transformation. The concept of evolution, as set forth in Lamarck's *Philosophie Zoologique* (Zoological Philosophy), 1809, had come into being. A trend led all living things to progressively higher levels of complexity. Life had developed without interruption from the beginning to the present day and new species evolved from pre-existing ones over time; none died out completely. Efforts to adapt to changing habitats and living conditions, Lamarck reasoned, brought about changes in animals that were transmitted to successive generations (inheritance of acquired characteristics). That would account for the diversification of life as we see it today. But because these changes took place very gradually, they were undetectable from the human point of view.

Posterity was to endorse in general terms the concept of evolution, but controversy surrounded Lamarck's views on how it operated. Cuvier was influential in discrediting Lamarck's theory.

Cuvier vehemently opposed Lamarck's 'transformism', as his theory of evolution was called. Below, a 1792 journal of natural history.

JOURNAL
D'HISTOIRE NATURELLE;

Rédigé par MM. LAMARCK, BRUGUIÈRE, OLIVIER, HAÜY et PELLETIER.

TOME PREMIER

PARIS.

de l'Imprimerie du Cercle atre-François, N°. 4.

1792.

ME DE LA LIBERTÉ.

Blind and alone, Lamarck (above) died in 1829. In less than twenty years his work was to become a source of Darwin's theories.

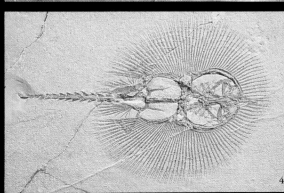

Fossils of the sea

1 *Aeduella blainvillei*, an actinopterygian (ray-finned fish) found in Autun, France (Permian, about 225 million years ago). Actinopterygians, of which the majority of living fish are representative, date back to Palaeozoic times. The thick, shiny scales of this specimen are perfectly preserved.

2 *Proteroctopus ribeit*, the oldest known octopus, from the Jurassic period (150 million years ago). In this astonishing example of fossilization, the internal organs, arms and suckers have all been preserved.

3 Fossil-bearing sedimentary rock (Miocene, 20 million years ago) built up from the remains of marine organisms and shell fragments, from a bay in France that once extended far inland. Small colonies of bryozoans (invertebrates that reproduce by budding), with their distinctive fanlike branching, are visible in this greatly enlarged photograph.

4 *Cyclobatis*, a selachian, or cartilaginous fish, from Sahel Alma, Lebanon (Cretaceous, 70 million years ago). The body is completely surrounded by the circular imprint of its highly developed pectoral fins.

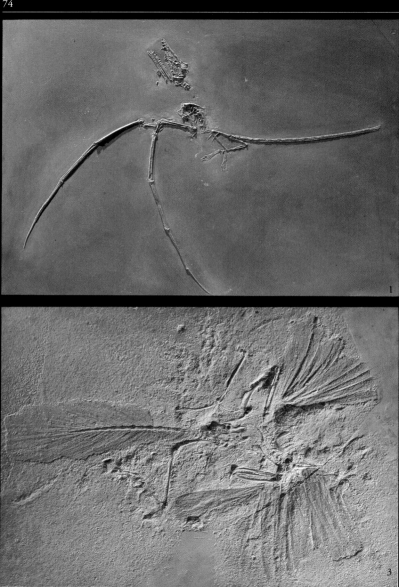

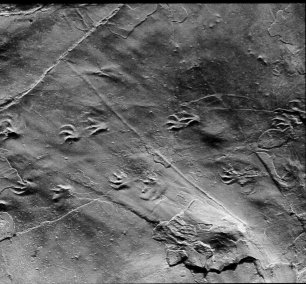

Fossils of the air

1 *Campylognathus,* a flying reptile, or pterosaur, from the fine-grained shale of Bavaria (Jurassic, 136 million years ago). It used its enormous wings to glide through the air; a flesh-eater, it fed on fish snatched on the wing.

2 *Palaeortyx,* a bird from the gypsum of Montmartre (Eocene, 45 million years ago). During this period, lagoons supporting a great many land- and water-dwelling faunas dotted the region surrounding Paris.

3 *Archaeopteryx,* one of the earliest birds, from Bavaria (Jurassic, 150 million years ago). An intermediate form, it not only had certain reptilian features (teeth, claws, long tail) but, as we can see in this beautifully preserved specimen, a bird's wing structure and feathers.

4 Footprints left by small primitive amphibians, the stegocephalians, in the ooze of a swamp (Permian, 225 million years ago) in southern France.

4

Fossils of the land

1 *Tarbosaurus,* from Mongolia (Cretaceous, 80 million years ago), was a meat-eating dinosaur related to the tyrannosaurs of North America. International teams of fossil hunters regularly descend upon central Mongolia, a veritable 'graveyard' of fossil vertebrates.

2 Skull of *Smilodon* found in Brazil (Pliocene, 2.5 million years ago), the sabre-toothed tiger of America. It used its huge, dagger-like upper canines to slice through prey.

3 *Seymouria baylorensis,* an amphibian from Texas (Carboniferous, 290 million years ago), lived in coal-bearing lagoons. This fossilized individual was caught as it walked along the bottom of a mudhole.

4 Skull of *Adapis magnus,* found in the phosphate rock strata of Quercy, France (Eocene, 45 million years ago). The Adapidae, of which there are no living representatives, belonged to the same group as humans – the primates.

The age of fossils and the Earth is now calculated in millions, not thousands, of years

Abandoning his studies in law at Oxford for a career in geology, Charles Lyell (1797–1875) published his *Principles of Geology* in 1830; it soon became the essential textbook of the profession. Starting from Lamarck's ideas, it also built on the observations of James Hutton (1726-97) whose *Theory of the Earth* (1795) had been attacked for discrediting the Scriptures. With Lyell's book came acceptance of Hutton's ideas, that geological transformations resulted from gradual changes spanning millions of years and that we can understand the past by examining current processes. Lyell redefined geological time and brought it more in line with current estimates. Also in *Principles of Geology* Lyell first proposed the name *palaeontology* (in Greek, 'the science of early beings') for the study of fossils and past geological periods.

Lyell held that the earth's history is subject to cyclical variations. Therefore, he argued in *Principles of Geology,* it stood to reason that one day extinct species might live again, that 'the huge iguanodon might reappear in the woods, and the ichthyosaur in the sea, while the pterodactyl might flit again through umbrageous groves of tree-ferns'.

Below: Charles Lyell, centre, facing Charles Darwin.

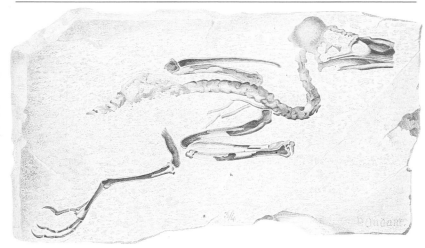

Fossils helped Alcide Dessalines d'Orbigny (1802–57) shed new light on the sequence of geological strata

In 1834 French naturalist d'Orbigny returned from a journey to South America with an impressive body of observations and material pertaining to everything from ethnology to geology. Of particular importance was a group of fossils which comprised the first major palaeontological collection from South America.

Eventually d'Orbigny's collection boasted over a hundred thousand items; he described some eighteen thousand invertebrate species in his *Prodrome de Paléontologie Stratigraphique* (Prodromus to Stratigraphic Palaeontology). Scientists before him had noted that some fossils occurred only in certain layers of a geological formation. D'Orbigny arranged them into a sequence of twenty-seven stratigraphic stages, each with its particular fossils. These subdivisions would be the founding of the science of stratigraphical palaeontology and are still used today. However, d'Orbigny mistakenly espoused Cuvier's concept of fixed species and worked out a sequence of twenty-seven catastrophes, one for each stage – the last being the Biblical Flood.

D'Orbigny (below) was sent on an expedition to South America after his early palaeontological studies appeared in print in 1825. He subsequently specialized in stratigraphic palaeontology and in 1869 published *Atlas de d'Orbigny*, which included his own drawing of a fossil bird found in a Paris quarry (above).

Fronds of a fossil fern
(below) and
reconstruction of a tree
fern (right) from Adolphe
Brongniart's *Histoire des
Végétaux Fossiles* (History
of Fossil Plants), 1828–37.

A caricature of Darwin,
opposite.

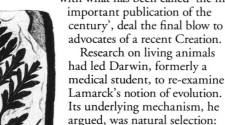

The idea of evolution is introduced into the field of biology

It was a contemporary of Lyell and d'Orbigny, English
naturalist Charles Robert Darwin (1809–82), who would,
with what has been called 'the most
important publication of the
century', deal the final blow to
advocates of a recent Creation.

Research on living animals
had led Darwin, formerly a
medical student, to re-examine
Lamarck's notion of evolution.
Its underlying mechanism, he
argued, was natural selection:
Only those animals best adapted
to their environment do not
succumb to it and are able to
survive. In 1859 Darwin
published *On the Origin of Species
by Means of Natural Selection: Or
the Preservation of Favoured Races
in the Struggle for Life,* which
immediately sent shock waves
through the scientific
community. Some
were receptive to the
new theory; others,
especially the
theologically
inclined,
erupted

with righteous indignation. The outcry against him peaked when, in *The Descent of Man and Selection in Relation to Sex* (1871), Darwin asserted that humans were part of the animal world and assigned them a place near the apes. Darwin's theories, which ignited an explosive mixture of astonishment, anger and resentment, were to have a tremendous impact on religion and science alike. Humans could now be incorporated into nature and assume their true biological place within it. The first fossil human remains came to light in the second half of the 19th century. The evolutionist view of the world was to revolutionize, not just modern science, but every facet of contemporary thought.

While Darwin did not exactly deny the existence of God, his wife is said to have despaired that 'God is being moved farther and farther from us.' The proposition that *Homo sapiens* had been created in God's image was a fundamental precept of Chistianity. As it would be ludicrous to imagine the Creator looking like a tadpole or even an ape, one could only infer from Darwin's theory of evolution that humans had not been created in God's image. Charges of heresy and atheism were lodged against Darwin and his followers.

THE LONDON SKETCH BOOK.

PROF. DARWIN.

This is the ape of form.
Love's Labor Lost, act 5, scene 2.

Some four or five descents since.
All's Well that Ends Well, act 3, sc. 7.

The spotlight now shifted to the dinosaurs, or 'terrible lizards', giants which ruled the earth for 160 million years, then suddenly – with no apparent explanation – died out.

CHAPTER 4

THE MONARCHS OF PREHISTORY

Thomas Hawkins, a rather eccentric English collector, illustrated *The Book of Great Sea-Dragons* (1840, illustration opposite). In the early 19th century, duels like this one between an ichthyosaur (center) and two plesiosaurs sustained the nightmares of a tortured generation. Part of an iguanodon skeleton, right.

Marine reptiles from Jurassic times – *Mosasaurus* and, by the early 1800s, the *Ichthyosaurus* ('lizard fish') and *Plesiosaurus* ('close to lizards') – were the first such creatures to be identified.

In 1824 Lyell's mentor, the Reverend William Buckland, publishes the first description of a 'terrible lizard' for the London Geological Society

The Oxford mineralogist who had inspired Lyell to give up law for geology, Buckland was a colourful character and an outstanding scientist. He based his findings, published as 'Notice on the *Megalosaurus* or Great Fossil Lizard of Stonesfield', on part of a lower jaw, a number of vertebrae, an incomplete pelvis and shoulder blade, and several bones from a hind limb that were on display in a block of slate at the Oxford University Museum. Some of the animal's features were lizardlike, others crocodilian. Yet he felt certain it was neither a lizard nor a crocodile. In any event, it was a creature of staggering size 'compared with the ordinary standard of the lizard family'. As Buckland pointed out, 'A length exceeding forty feet [12 metres] and a bulk equal to that of an elephant seven feet high [over two metres] have been assigned by Cuvier to the individual to which this bone belonged.' Nothing like it had ever been imagined.

Attention now shifts to land reptiles: Gideon Algernon Mantell (1790–1857) describes the *Iguanodon* the following year

Mantell was a physician – and a glutton for work. When he was not with his patients, he studied the fossil bones that cluttered his residence in the English village of Lewes. He often made house calls, and as he made his rounds by horse and carriage he kept his eyes riveted on the side of the road. He was constantly on the lookout for fossils. Mantell's wife, Mary Ann, shared in his enthusiasm; she contributed the 364 drawings that would accompany Mantell's 1822 treatise, *The Fossils of the South Downs.*

One day in 1822, while Mary Ann was waiting for him outside a patient's house, she spotted something shiny in a pile of stone rubble that had been left for road

Buckland sought tirelessly to prove that fossils resulted from the Biblical Flood and slanted all his findings to fit this hypothesis. For example, when he found a rhinoceros skeleton preserved whole beside some cattle and deer bones (below, an engraving from his *Reliquiae Diluvianae,* 1823), he maintained that diluvial waters had swept the animal into a pit, which was then filled in with mud and pebbles.

Lead Vein

repairs. She picked up the stone. She could not have guessed how momentous that simple act was to prove. The stone contained a fossil tooth. Mary Ann Mantell had just discovered the first piece of an animal that posterity would know as *Iguanodon*. (But her husband's 'obsessive reptilomania' was to prove too much for her: fifteen years later she left with their four children.)

Mantell was intrigued by the unusual tooth and resolved to learn more about it. With the help of some quarriers (whom he paid generously), he discovered a number of bones belonging to what he described as an 'unknown colossal herbivorous reptile' and announced his findings to the London Geological Society. Mantell was not daunted by the prospect continuing alone. He knew he had found the fragments of a reptile.

Mantell (above) exhibited his collection of palaeontological specimens in his house in the village of Lewes, where he practised medicine. In 1833 he moved his family and fossils into a spacious house in nearby Brighton, on the shore. He sold his 'museum' to the British Museum for £4000 in 1838, the year his *Wonders of Geology* first appeared in print. Bereft of his beloved fossils, Mantell, the discoverer of dinosaurs, died in 1852 in London a broken man. Today a brass plate on his residence in Lewes proclaims, 'He discovered the *Iguanodon.*'

PRIMARY SERIES

TERTIARY SERIES AND EXTINCT VOLCANOES

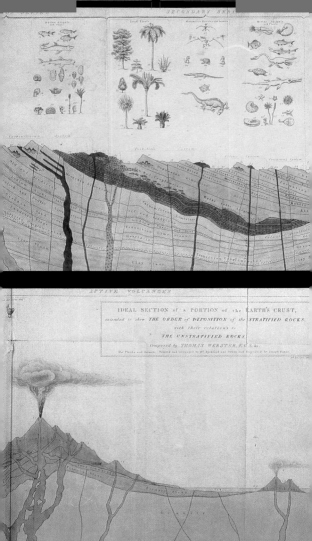

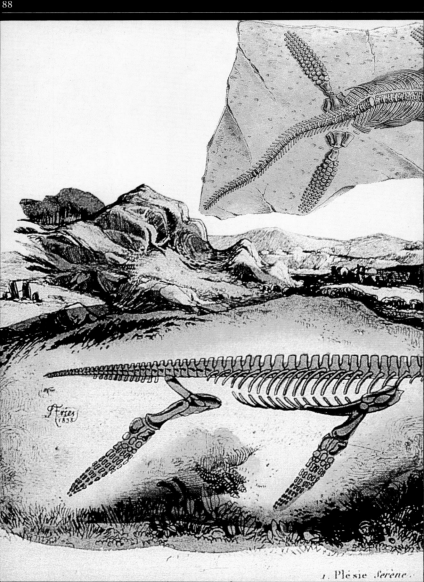

1. Plésie Serène.

Sea dragons

W ith the discovery of the first marine reptiles – ichthyosaurs (above) and plesiosaurs (below) – dragons made a dramatic comeback in literature.

❛ The fight began two hundred yards from the raft. We could distinctly see the two adversaries....

'He's right!... The first of those monsters has the snout of a porpoise, the head of a lizard, and the teeth of a crocodile. He's the most formidable of the primeval marine reptiles: the ichthyosaur!'

'And the other one?'

'The other one is a serpent with a turtle's shell, the mortal enemy of the first one: the plesiosaur!'

Hans was right....
Before my eyes were two reptiles of the primordial oceans.❜

Jules Verne,
Journey to the Centre of the Earth, 1864

He pressed on with his palaeontological detective work. Tooth and bones in hand, he went to the Hunterian Museum of the Royal College of Surgeons in London – its collection of material pertaining to animal anatomy was the most extensive of its day – and rummaged through drawer after drawer of reptilian bones and teeth. He found nothing comparable to his specimens. Mantell showed his treasures to Samuel Stutchbury, who – an incredible stroke of luck – happened to be in the museum investigating the iguana. Off he dashed to fetch an iguana skeleton. Mantell's tooth matched the iguana's, only it was much larger! Proof that Mantell had been right about the animal's identity all along.

In 1825, Mantell's 'Notice on the *Iguanodon,* a Newly Discovered Fossil Reptile, from the Sandstone of Tilgate Forest, in Sussex' appeared in *Philosophical Transactions of the Royal Society.* Solving the riddle had taken three years of work, three years of friendly but intense debate. Cuvier, Buckland and other experts concurred with his opinion.

Nine years later, in 1834, the largely complete, if disarticulated skeleton of a young *Iguanodon* was chiselled out of a quarry at Maidstone, Kent. Mantell adjusted his reconstruction accordingly. Back in 1825 he had described it as an iguana-like quadruped with a small horn on its snout. By 1851 he would state that 'unlike the rest of its class, the *Iguanodon* had the body supported as in the mammalia, and the abdomen suspended higher from the ground than in any existing saurians.'

In 1841, at a meeting of the British Association for the Advancement of Science, a collective name for land-dwelling fossil reptiles is proposed: dinosaurs

More discoveries were made in the wake of Mantell's and Buckland's research. By 1841 a total of nine Mesozoic reptilian genera had been described, two of them by English palaeontologist Richard Owen (1804–92).

A consummate anatomist, Owen compared these fossil reptiles with living counterparts and concluded that they

Richard Owen (in a c. 1840 photograph, opposite) was born in Lancaster in 1804. After studying general medicine, he completely devoted himself to anatomy. Appointed a professor in 1836, he went on to publish many books and became one of the foremost scientists in Great Britain. He was a personal friend of Queen Victoria's.

In 1841 Owen described two fossil reptiles, one from the Triassic, the other from the Jurassic and, during a meeting in Plymouth, suggested that these peculiar creatures be collectively referred to as 'dinosaurs'. The word first appeared in print in 1842. An 1857 lithograph of Owen giving a lecture (left).

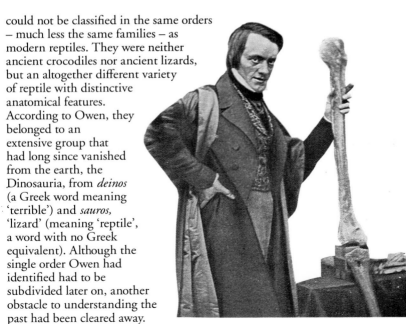

could not be classified in the same orders – much less the same families – as modern reptiles. They were neither ancient crocodiles nor ancient lizards, but an altogether different variety of reptile with distinctive anatomical features. According to Owen, they belonged to an extensive group that had long since vanished from the earth, the Dinosauria, from *deinos* (a Greek word meaning 'terrible') and *sauros,* 'lizard' (meaning 'reptile', a word with no Greek equivalent). Although the single order Owen had identified had to be subdivided later on, another obstacle to understanding the past had been cleared away.

The Crystal Palace: bringing the dead back to life

What had all these animals looked like when their skeletons were wrapped in flesh and sheathed in skin? Until then, no one had ventured anything beyond skeletal reconstruction. In the mid-1800s Owen, now a leading figure in British science, was put in charge of a project to build life-size, three-dimensional reconstructions of large fossil animals.

In 1854 an extensive park in which sightseers could stroll among dinosaurs, ichthyosaurs and plesiosaurs – not to mention hypothetical mammals and crocodiles concocted by Owen with the help of sculptor Benjamin Waterhouse Hawkins – opened in the London suburb of Sydenham, where the Crystal Palace, originally constructed in Hyde Park, had recently been re-erected.

To mark the occasion, an iguanodon was the guest of honour at a very

The invitations for the dinner party at the Crystal Palace bore a decorative engraving of the banquet table inside a reconstructed iguanodon (above).

unusual banquet shortly before opening day.
A table was set up in the belly of the reconstructed
creature, with Owen enthroned in its head and
Hawkins and some twenty other guests seated
along either side.

We have since learned that these reconstructions
were seriously flawed. *Iguanodon,* for example, turned
out to be a classic biped with a pair of sturdy hind legs,
short, thick-set 'arms', and a thumb spike – the horn
which Owen had placed at the tip of the snout – on
each of its hands.

But these facts did not come to light until the discovery
of the spectacular Bernissart fossil beds twenty years
later. Until then, the only available clues about
Iguanodon and its kin, dinosaurian or
otherwise, were partial skeletons,
making accurate reconstruction
difficult at best.

The Exposition of
1851 in Hyde
Park, London, proved
so popular that its
architectural centrepiece,
the Crystal Palace, was
re-erected in a London
suburb; a surrounding
park was designed as a
setting for the fauna of
prehistoric England.
Painter and sculptor
Benjamin Waterhouse
Hawkins built these
dinosaurs (below, a
lithograph of the
scene) under
Owen's supervision.

A spectacular find: Bernissart

In 1877 some fossils were discovered in the coal mines at Bernissart, Belgium, but the find went virtually unnoticed. The following year, miners working almost 300 metres below the surface unwittingly dug a shaft through the skeleton of a huge animal, all but destroying it before they realized what they had done. In what was to become a classic sequence of events, the workers reported the find to the director of the mine, who in turn notified the Institut Royal des Sciences in Brussels, which in turn dispatched Dr Pierre-Joseph van Beneden (1809–94), a distinguished Belgian palaeontologist, to the site. He identified the bones as the remains of iguanodons – lots and lots of iguanodons. Nothing like it had ever been seen before.

The Bernissart sensation was never to be repeated anywhere else in the world. Equally productive sites – and not just in terms of dinosaurs – may lie hidden beneath the Old and New Worlds, but urbanization is hampering efforts to find them. Economic development has been a boon to palaeontology, but it has also worked to its detriment. Every time ground is broken for a mine, a quarry, or for construction projects like railroads and highways, there is a good chance that fossil remains will be unearthed. If, however, proper procedures are not followed, vestiges of prehistoric life can be destroyed – and frequently are. There may not always be a worker in the mine or quarry who knows enough to notify a supervisor, a supervisor who knows enough to notify a palaeontologist, a scientific institution, or even an amateur fossil hunter. Lastly, the use of modern equipment that can quickly scoop out tremendous amounts of earth all but rules out the time-consuming and delicate process of hunting for fossils.

The Bernissart fossil beds yielded at least ten complete iguanodon skeletons and many partial skeletons. How did these animals come to perish all at once? This region of Belgium 120 million years ago was swampland where herds of these huge, plant-eating creatures flourished in the warm, humid climate. Did the iguanodons flee from some danger, only to find themselves mired in a patch of loose, shifting ground? Were they compelled by a dry spell to go off in search of water, only to sink in the ooze of a now-vanished shoreline? We may never know.

The Bernissart skeletons are now on display at the Royal Institute in Brussels.

Gone were the days of fanciful monsters. But fact was proving stranger than fiction: dinosaurs were bigger than some of the biggest human giants. Palaeontology was on its way to solving the last remaining riddles; in this race to unlock mysteries, everybody was at the starting line, scientists and inquisitive amateurs alike.

CHAPTER 5
AMATEURS AND PROFESSIONALS

Worker and artist in the service of palaeontology: a miner discovering a primeval forest deep inside a shaft (right) and illustrator Charles R. Knight, whose reconstructions (opposite, a mammoth) helped bring vanished animals back to life.

An amateur (literally, 'one who loves') has a fondness for something in particular and by definition does not engage in his or her pursuit as a profession. The ranks of amateur palaeontologists swelled in the 1800s. Granted, previous centuries could also claim their share of amateurs, but they were a different breed, intrigued not just by fossils but by natural phenomena in general, as evidenced by the eclecticism of their collections.

Like virtually every other subject discussed at the time, fossils were often placed within a broader context of philosophical speculation. The 19th century witnessed the emergence of individuals who made palaeontology their one and only pastime, who filled every spare moment tracking down, studying, and writing about fossils. They made a vital contribution to the development of this fledgling discipline.

Some inspired amateurs would become the palaeontology 'Establishment'

Not all of the leading lights of 19th-century palaeontology were professionals – far from it. Mantell was, and remained, a country doctor. Hermann von Meyer, founder of *Palaeontographia* (one of the first journals devoted solely to palaeontology) and noted authority on fossil reptiles,

One hundred million years ago, plesiosaurs battled it out in the pitiless world of what is now northeastern Texas. Some buried treasure unexpectedly turned up in a field on a farm near Dallas belonging to a Mr Tidwell (left). Palaeontology relies heavily on such chance finds – hence, the importance of amateurs and the attendant risk that a site might fall victim to plunder.

In the English press, scientists and fossils were front-page news – and grist for the caricaturist's mill (below, a trilobite).

was a financial officer for the German parliament and worked his way up to administrative director. To safeguard his independence, he even turned down an offer to teach at the University of Göttingen.

The church, too, helped swell the ranks of those intrigued by the 'science of past life'. Witness the Reverend Buckland, or Abbé Croizet, the vicar of a hamlet in central France. When not ministering to his flock, Croizet tended to the fossils in his parish, for in these 'stony animals' he saw tangible evidence of the ongoing Creation.

In fact, many scientists who held positions in the palaeontology 'establishment' – professors, museum department heads and the like – began their careers as amateurs.

In 1869 Edouard-Armand Lartet (1801–71) of France, a pioneer in the methodical excavation of fossil-bearing sediments and in human palaeontology, was appointed professor of palaeontology at the Museum of Natural History in Paris. Before that, however, he practised law – a profession with no apparent connection to the study of prehistoric organisms. But the fossil tooth destined to set him on the road to becoming one of the founders of palaeontology was the gift of a grateful farmer who had gone to him for legal advice.

In 1873 a complete skeleton of *Elephas meridionalis,* mired upright in a swamp a million years ago, was discovered in southern France. Excavating the animal (above, a lithograph of the excavation team) was a very delicate procedure, and its fossil bones had to be reinforced as work progressed. It is now on display in the Museum of Natural History in Paris. This probiscidean, which predated the less bulky mammoth, lived in a hot climate that made fur unnecessary.

Fossil hunting in faraway places

A number of palaeontologists – including Sir Richard
Owen and Othniel Charles Marsh – confined themselves
to laboratory work. They described, analysed, and
interpreted the specimens that others collected in the
field. Many others, however, positively revelled in on-site
excavation: Mantell in his native England, Edward
Drinker Cope in the United States, Albert Gaudry in
Greece and d'Orbigny in South America.

It was a pleasure they shared with legions of amateur
fossil hunters, a pleasure that gave professional and non-
professional alike the fortitude to become miners
if necessary, to burrow many metres underground,
to pick and scrape away at earth and rock for hours on
end in scorching heat or torrential rain, to trudge along
mile after mile of what passed for trails, to go up and
down, up and down – without flagging. In short, to
lead as much the life of a ditchdigger as of a starchily
attired scientist.

Both amateur and professional palaeontologists relied
on informants in the quarries and mines, who duly
notified them of discoveries. Labourers whose occupation
kept them constantly in the field were essential to

The first
palaeontologist to
travel to distant sites,
d'Orbigny was twenty-
four years old when he set
sail for South America in
1826. The next eight
years took him from
Amazonia to Patagonia
and from the Atlantic to
the Pacific. Braving every
danger imaginable, he
returned with an
extraordinary body of
material pertaining to
disciplines as diverse as
geology, natural history
and ethnology. A chair of
palaeontology at the
Museum of Natural
History in Paris was
established expressly for
him in 1853. Above: A
lithograph based on one
of d'Orbigny's drawings.

their work. They still are. Had it not been for them, the Great Animal of Maastricht, the iguanodons of Bernissart and countless other fossils might never have come to light.

Enter the dealers

Not all amateurs acted from unselfish motives. Burgeoning interest in fossils fostered a full-blown business. Museums and individual palaeontologists were on the lookout for more and more specimens to study. People living near fossil-bearing sediments soon realized that these formations were potential sources of substantial income. There was a clientele; there would be dealers.

The most celebrated fossil brokers were the Annings of Lyme Regis on the southwest coast of England, a region rich in Mesozoic marine reptiles. The head of the family, Richard Anning, began selling his finds to visitors in the late 1700s to supplement his income. After his death his children, Joseph and Mary, recruited their little dog and adopted a more systematic approach to the family business.

Mary and her dog routinely went out for walks along the coastal bluffs, especially after storms that caused rockfalls, and scanned the exposed sediments for fossils. She then sold what she found to dukes, barons, and other members of the British peerage who felt fashion-bound to take an interest in palaeontology. (In most cases, they donated or bequeathed their holdings to the British Museum.)

Mary, who later became a naturalist, and her dog were remarkably sharp-eyed fossil hunters. They are credited with discovering the first skeleton to be identified as an ichthyosaur, which anatomy professor

The first *Archaeopteryx* fossil ever discovered (1860) came from a quarry at Solnhofen, Germany. The original owner of the specimen sold it to the British Museum for £700. Another skeleton turned up in 1877. A private collector paid 140 German marks for it, but this extremely rare bird was resold almost at once to the Humboldt Museum of the University of Berlin – for over one hundred times that amount! This 1941 painting of an *Archaeopteryx* (below) is by Zdeněk Burian.

Mary Anning (left) combed the English coast for fossils. Whenever she found one, she would leave her dog behind to mark the spot and return with reinforcements to dig out the fossil remains. A martyr to science, the poor animal was crushed to death in a rockfall.

On 15 June 1908, the day the *Diplodocus* was unveiled, a gala 'banquet' was held in the main palaeontology gallery of the Museum of Natural History, Paris. The menu (below) lists Albert Gaudry Soup, Palaeontological Hors d'Oeuvres, Oligocene Sole from Aix, Saddle of Entelodont with Perrier Sauce, Volcanic Bombe, and desserts.

Sir Everard Home purchased for £23. As word of the creature spread, prices soared. Four years later, another ichthyosaur specimen was auctioned off for £150. In 1824 the Duke of Buckingham parted with the same sum for the nearly complete skeleton of a plesiosaur – still unidentified at the time – that Mary and her dog had found on another occasion. Incomplete specimens could be had more cheaply. A bid of £10 was all Cuvier needed to claim an ichthyosaur's femur.

A less profit-minded man, a grocer by the name of Atthey, lived in Newcastle, in the heart of England's mining district. Miners brought their fossil finds to him, and he would trade them for goods and study them whenever there was a lull in business. Mr Atthey eschewed a potential fortune and was even forced into bankruptcy, but his work gained the lasting respect of scientists.

In Germany Bernhard Hauff refined the fossil-selling business. Beginning in the 1890s he prepared fossil skeletons, reconstructed them on the slab of shale in

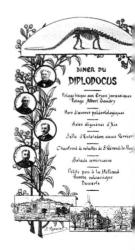

DINER DU
DIPLODOCUS

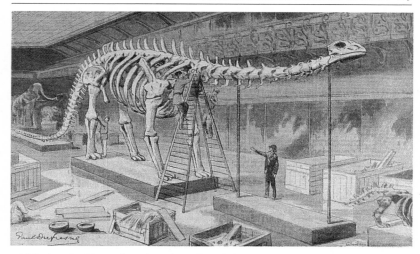

which they had been found, and marketed them as 'ready-to-use' specimens. His laboratory was well stocked with crocodilians, plesiosaurs, pterosaurs, fishes and invertebrates of all kinds. But ichthyosaurs were the highlight of his collection; and it was one of his fossils that led to the discovery that this reptile had back and tail fins.

Patronage in flower

While some merely speculated in fossils, others with greater wealth at their command spent small fortunes on them. The patrons of palaeontology came into their own during the 19th century.

Bankers and captains of industry financed everything from expeditions and collections to entire museums, especially in the United States. Steel magnate and fossil enthusiast Andrew Carnegie (1835–1919) founded a museum in Pittsburgh that soon became internationally famous, notably for its dinosaurs. In the early 1900s a team from the Carnegie Museum discovered a spectacular concentration of Mesozoic reptiles at a spot in Utah that came to be known as Carnegie Quarry (now Dinosaur National Monument). Carnegie funded years of excavation at the site and

In 1907 American philanthropist Andrew Carnegie decided to donate a plaster cast of *Diplodocus carnegiei* to France as a token of friendship between the two countries. In April 1908, thirty-four crates of disassembled pieces arrived in Paris. Professor W. J. Holland and his assistant came from America to supervise the mounting of the specimen (above).

The natural history division of the British Museum (left) boasted major fossil collections when it opened in 1880. The Palaeontology Gallery in Paris (opposite) opened its doors to the public on 21 July 1898 and proved an immediate success, drawing eleven thousand visitors on the first Sunday alone.

Discovered in Madagascar and displayed at the Museum of Natural History in Paris, *Aepyornis* (literally, 'lofty bird', below) stood nearly 2.68 metres tall.

donated plaster casts of the Carnegie Museum's star attraction, *Diplodocus carnegiei,* to museums in London, Paris, Berlin, Vienna, Bologna, La Plata and Mexico City. Other wealthy tycoons, such as steel magnate Henry Clay Frick, kept up the tradition by lavishing a portion of their enormous wealth on the science of vanished animal species.

Another case in point: American George Peabody, the prominent financier, provided his nephew, Othniel Charles Marsh, with the funds he needed for schooling and research. He also subsidized colleges, universities, and three museums, including those at Yale and Harvard universities that now bear his name.

Soon every major city boasts a natural history museum with a highly respected palaeontology department

With support flowing in from public coffers as well as private donations and bequests, museums could now afford to build up collections independently. Visitors came in droves. New buildings had to be opened and old ones expanded to house the accumulated finds of the 19th century. Once limited to shells, fishes and individual bones – simply because such specimens were easily accommodated – museum display areas were now invaded by gigantic skeletons that were far more graphic and much easier for the public to comprehend than all the rocks of yesteryear combined.

In the United States, newly founded museums briskly proceeded to amass collections worthy of America's fossil riches. The Peabody Museum at Yale, the Carnegie Museum in Pittsburgh, the National Museum of Natural History in Washington, D.C., and, above all, the American Museum of Natural History in New York City were the driving force behind a number of incredible palaeontological adventures.

In 1880 the British Museum in London relocated its natural history collection to new quarters in South Kensington. In 1898 a palaeontology gallery opened in Paris. German museums in Frankfurt, Berlin and Stuttgart underwent comparable expansion.

These museums boasted on-premises laboratories, conducted independent research, and had specimens shipped in, often from distant localities. One writer reports that by the end of the century the Bavarian State Collection in Munich had obtained fossils from Argentina, Uruguay, the United States, Greece, England and Egypt.

Artists help re-create 'period' environments of vanished species

Attracting throngs to museums required more than putting fossils on display. Visitors wanted to see reconstructions that were not only scientifically sound but enjoyable to look at. To this end, artists were brought in to work under the supervision of palaeontologists. Owen pioneered this trend in England with the fossil reconstructions in the Crystal Palace. A similar project in New York's Central Park that was to have been directed by Hawkins, Owen's collaborator and noted authority, fell through, a victim of underhand local politics.

Another emerging trend was to display all these vanished creatures, not in storm-whipped seas or disconcertingly murky landscapes, but amid the actual vegetation of the period they lived in. Fanciful though habitat reconstructions may have been on occasion, many illustrators such as American Charles R. Knight became masterful in the art of re-creating lost worlds.

The earliest representations of fossils – animal paintings or carvings in the Palaeolithic caves of Europe – date back to a time when some of the creatures we now know only as fossils were still alive. In the 16th–18th centuries reconstructions of vanished animals, from rhinoceroses to unicorns, were largely figments of the imagination. That all changed in the 19th century, when fossils became the basis for re-creating prehistoric life. The sculptures by Benjamin Waterhouse Hawkins (opposite, shown working on his Crystal Palace dinosaurs) and paintings by Charles R. Knight (above, a sea monster) were still approximations. The transition to anatomically correct reconstructions did not occur until the 20th century.

In the late 1800s, palaeontologists in North America were striking out into vast expanses of unpopulated territory. Once assumed to harbour the monstrous animals and human giants that had vanished from Europe, this region proved to be extraordinarily rich in fossils.

CHAPTER 6

AMERICAN PALAEONTOLOGY COMES OF AGE

Exploration of new regions provides an ever-increasing flow of material from the field. Here Norwegian palaeontologists, for example, have combed the Arctic island of Spitzbergen for fossils (left). Their crates have been filled with plaster casts of dinosaur bones and are ready to be shipped to the Paleontologisk Museum in Oslo. Opposite: A *Diplodocus* by Zdeněk Burian.

Excavations turned up several virtually intact skeletons – some gigantic – of animals that until then had been identified solely on the basis of fragments, or that no one had known even existed. These stupendous remains sent a surge of enthusiasm through the public and helped to broaden palaeontology's appeal beyond scientific circles.

Actually, the first discoveries in North America date back to the middle of the 18th century, when the wealthy and intellectual elite of American society developed the same passion for fossils that had overtaken their counterparts in Europe. Thomas Jefferson wrote about the history of extinct animals before he became president in 1801. In 1804, when Jefferson selected army officers Merriwether Lewis (1774–1809) and William Clark (1770–1838) to search out a land route to the Pacific, he reportedly instructed them to keep an eye out for living descendants of fossil creatures. But all Lewis and Clark could find were more fossils. Palaeontology did not make its first real thrust west of the Mississippi until the second half of the 19th century.

Major finds in the early 1800s are limited to the eastern United States

In 1801, with the help of the American Philosophical Society, portrait painter Charles Willson Peale (1741–1827), an avid collector of natural history specimens, started systematically excavating and sketching mastodon skeletons found in a peat bog in Orange County, New York. Elaborate mechanical contraptions were devised expressly for the project. Subsequent digs throughout the region turned up loose bits of fossil fishes, reptiles and mammals. When Edward Hitchcock, professor of 'theology and natural geology' at Amherst College (Massachusetts), found some fossil footprints in the Connecticut River valley, he assumed they had been made by birds 3 to 4 metres tall, or reptiles, or even marsupials.

A bit later, in 1858, University of Pennsylvania anatomy professor Joseph Leidy studied the remains of a dinosaur of the species *Hadrosaurus foulkii* (named

To his dying day, Edward Hitchcock believed that the footprints he had discovered in the Connecticut River valley were made by gigantic birds and identified them as such in the so-called Appleton Cabinet at Amherst College (opposite). What he had found were actually the

footprints of early dinosaurs, which proved to have a structure similar to that of birds.

after William Parker Foulke, who had supervised its excavation from the marl pits near Haddonfield, New Jersey). As it turned out, the animal's range was limited solely to North America.

Albert Koch, a German collector, motivated less by scientific curiosity than by the prospect of reaping profits from the fossil business, tried his hand at mounting animal remains that had been reclaimed from the earth. In 1832 he pieced together a huge skeleton out of some poorly preserved mastodon bones and exhibited the fantastic composite as the sea monster *Missourium,* the Leviathan of the Bible. The British Museum bought his find two years later and reassembled it into a specimen that more closely approximated its actual appearance.

Koch tried to repeat this success in 1844. This time he concocted a 35-metre-long sea serpent, *Hydrarchus sillimani,* out of the bones of at least five different individuals. This fabrication went on display in New York and cities throughout Europe before scientists exposed the forgery and Koch's career came to an end.

Joseph Leidy (below), the founder of vertebrate palaeontology in the United States, proudly poses next to a bone belonging to *Hadrosaurus,* the first dinosaur skeleton discovered in North America. Opposite: a 19th-century fossil hunter.

The setting is Orange County, New York; the time, the early 1800s. In 1799 John Masten came across a number of huge bones while cutting peat on his farm. With the help of a hundred or so neighbours, he dug into the ground and brought up some bones from the pit; but he went about it so hastily that they were all damaged. Two years later, Charles Willson Peale, a wealthy collector from Philadelphia, decided to step in. He leased Masten's peat bog for a hundred dollars. An elaborate contraption consisting of a pump and an enormous wheel were set up for the seemingly straightforward process of draining the pit. As curious throngs looked on, Peale brought up a mastodon skeleton, complete except for the lower jaw. Crews scoured nearby peat bogs for the missing piece. When a lower jaw with huge teeth finally did turn up, it seemed logical at the time to conclude that these awesome creatures were meat-eaters. We now know that the proboscideans, regardless of when they lived, were herbivorous. This is Peale's own depiction of the event.

The badlands of Nebraska, first stop along the road to winning the Far West

'Mauvaises terres' (literally, badlands) – that was what French trappers called this barren terrain of deeply eroded ravines and gullies ... the bane of farmers, but a dream come true for fossil hunters. As Joseph Leidy wrote in *Ancient Fauna of Nebraska,* 1853, 'The drooping spirits of the scorched geologist are not permitted, however, to flag. The fossil treasures of the way well repay its sultriness and fatigue. At every step, objects of the highest interest present themselves.'

Excavation yielded mammals large and small – in particular, remains of horses that shed new light on the early genealogy of their modern counterparts. People now realized that this and other regions just opening up to settlers might shelter vast amounts of such material.

The advance westward, interrupted by the Civil War, resumed on an even bigger scale after 1865. The restoration of peace ushered in a period of full-scale expeditions and systematic fossil-hunting campaigns.

Marsh (rear, centre), surrounded by rifle-toting students, ready to go dinosaur hunting.

The Dinosaur rush

The mighty transcontinental railroad led the way. Thousands of workers dug into the ground to lay track and gravel beds. As buried fossil remains might be unearthed at any moment, palaeontologists kept a sharp lookout.

Two dinosaur hunters left their mark on this epic undertaking. Othniel Charles Marsh and Edward Drinker Cope had first met in Europe; at a time when palaeontology was dominated by European scientists, it was not unusual for Americans to pursue their studies abroad. They became friends and even did some digging together after they returned to the United States in 1868. But relations between them quickly deteriorated into ruthless rivalry. Each was bent on reaching potential sites first, on making the most spectacular discoveries, and on securing exclusive rights by inducing workers to sign contracts on the spot. (In that respect, the far wealthier Marsh had the advantage.) At times they resorted to violence to

In 1877 a young schoolteacher by the name of Arthur Lakes discovered fossil bones of unprecedented size near Morrison, Colorado, and wrote to Marsh requesting financial assistance. Marsh sent him a cheque at once and dispatched his field collector, geology professor Benjamin Mudge of the Agricultural College of Kansas, to the site. Lakes was signed on as a member of Marsh's crew and sent to another site at Como Bluff, Wyoming (below), which two employees of the Union Pacific Railroad had found that very year.

prevent 'enemy troops' from encroaching on their turf. They waged an all-out war in print, making a major contribution to science in the process. In sheer volume, Cope outstripped his rival by far, 1200 articles to Marsh's 270. To get a head start on Marsh, Cope transmitted his findings by telegraph, resulting in highly erratic spellings of new species names – Cope has over a thousand to his credit – and incredibly muddled nomenclature. The feud intensified as they accused each other of pilfering fossils and antedating discoveries to secure priority. The press joined in the fray. Serious accusations, such as misappropriation of funds and political chicanery, were levelled against both sides. Only the death of the two rivals – Cope in 1897 and Marsh in 1899 – finally brought the war to an end.

Notification that a find had been made would come to Marsh or Cope by letter, preferably by telegraph. Agents were dispatched to the site to observe, evaluate and decide whether or not to start digging. Once they mustered field crews, which sometimes included complements of railroad workers or hired hands from

Relations were strained between Arthur Lakes and W. H. 'Bill' Reed, one-time big-game hunter and the man in charge at Como Bluff. Lakes approached the dig as a purely scientific undertaking and concentrated on drawing fossils and taking notes. Reed described him as lazy and accused him of spending more time wielding a brush than a pick. But were it not for Lakes' series of water-colours (above and previous page), we would have only a vague idea of what daily life was really like for these dinosaur hunters. The one above shows Professor Mudge examining a fresh find.

nearby ranches, the actual process of removing material got under way. It was tough going. Winter and summer, chunks of rock containing fossil remains had to be pulled out by hand, sometimes in punishing weather. One of Marsh's men, Arthur Lakes, reported he was 'at the bottom of a narrow pit 20 feet deep into which drift snow keeps blowing and fingers benumbed with cold from thermo between 20 and 30 degrees below zero and snow blowing blindingly down and covering up a bone as fast as it is unearthed.' Another entry from his journal, dated 9 August 1879: 'Storm and gales: hailstones the size of eggs.'

The material then had to be hauled out by covered wagon to the nearest river or railway line; from there the precious cargo was shipped back East. The entire operation required delicate handling. The fossils had to be protected, and sturdy craft were specially designed to withstand the weight of the rocks. Even so, wrecks were not always avoidable.

There were also Indians to reckon with, and, to make headway, crews had to take advantage of their seasonal

Judging by the watercolour which Arthur Lakes entitled *The Pleasures of Science,* the artist (standing) and his assistant found life at Como Bluff anything but pleasurable in February 1879. Winter after winter, this site yielded tons of fossils that were shipped back to Marsh in New Haven.

and tactical migrations, or resort to cunning. Cope is said to have curried favour with them by taking out his false teeth and putting them back in his mouth! Never having seen removable teeth before, the fascinated natives insisted he repeat the process a number of

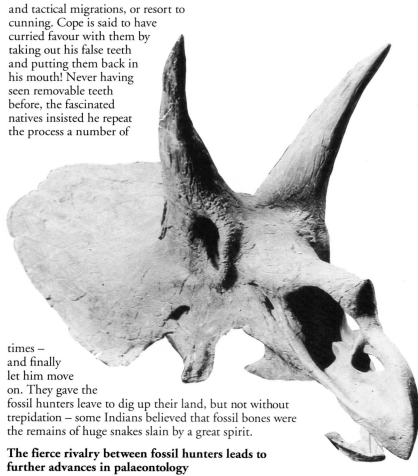

times – and finally let him move on. They gave the fossil hunters leave to dig up their land, but not without trepidation – some Indians believed that fossil bones were the remains of huge snakes slain by a great spirit.

The fierce rivalry between fossil hunters leads to further advances in palaeontology

As they raced to outdo each other, Marsh and Cope unearthed a treasure trove of fossil deposits. Marsh found a ten-kilometre stretch of well-preserved dinosaur bones at Como Bluff, Wyoming; Cope excavated along the Judith River in Montana; and both of them boasted noteworthy discoveries in Colorado. Through their efforts, hitherto unknown dinosaur species came to light.

Triceratops, a horned dinosaur measuring 9 metres long, lived in Canada and the western United States in the Late Cretaceous period. Marsh first identified it as a species of giant bison.

Dinosaur bones collected by famous New York palaeontologist Barnum Brown and his crew being hauled out of the Red Deer River site in Alberta in 1912. The area is now part of Canada's Alberta Dinosaur Park. The old wagon trail has been replaced by an asphalt road.

Palaeontologists– from the American Museum of Natural History in New York wrapping huge dinosaur vertebrae in plaster-soaked burlap strips at Nine Mile Quarry, Como Bluff, Wyoming, prior to boxing and shipping. Rice paste was also used to stiffen the bandages.

Barnum Brown at work at the Red Deer River site. In this photograph from 1912, we see him excavating a skeleton of *Corythosaurus,* a large Late Cretaceous duck-billed dinosaur with a tall, bony, laterally flattened skull crest.

This primeval seascape (1941) by Zdeněk Burian features a battle between two mosasaurs, fierce carnivorous swimming reptiles about 8 metres long which propelled their huge bodies through the water by swinging their mighty tails. A number of pteranodons glide overhead. The biggest flying reptiles of all time – some measured nearly 16 metres across – they fed on fish, plucking their prey from the sea while on the wing. The weight of their enormous beaks was counterbalanced by an odd excrescence reaching back from the skull. Like the dinosaurs, both of these reptiles died out in the Late Cretaceous.

Allosaurus, Brontosaurus, Diplodocus, and *Triceratops,* are but a few of the many species Cope or Marsh personally discovered and described. Most, if not all, of the leading North American palaeontologists of the 20th century started out under their tutelage and carried on their work – usually a great deal more peaceably.

Soon palaeontologists were prospecting all over the world

Another front opened along the Red Deer River in Alberta in the final decade of the 19th century. Then came Carnegie Quarry in Utah (now Dinosaur National Monument). Here visitors can watch as prehistoric animals are coaxed out of the exposed cliff face, exactly where they died millions of years ago.

Not a single continent has escaped palaeontological scrutiny; most recently, the Arctic and Antarctica have been added to the list.

This palaeontological epic has reaped an impressive bounty of fossils ranging from entire skeletons and the usual assortment of bones, shells and plants to mineralized skin, fossilized faeces (coprolites), footprints, and rain prints. Palaeontologists are using this evidence of the presence of life – and of the successive forms it has adopted over geological time – to reconstruct the history of our planet and the organisms which have lived on it.

A new era

The remains of large vertebrates have been in the limelight for some time, but smaller fossils have not been overlooked. They, too, have a part to play – a significant part at that – not only in our quest for the past but in modern life: certain shells, for example, can be crucial in the search for new oil deposits.

Today's ultra-sophisticated techniques have made it possible to detect minute traces of single-

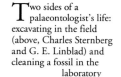

Two sides of a palaeontologist's life: excavating in the field (above, Charles Sternberg and G. E. Linblad) and cleaning a fossil in the laboratory (below).

celled organisms, such as bacteria and algae, in formations dating as far back as the Precambrian (3500 million years ago), a period previously thought to be devoid of life.

The 19th century resurrected a world of enormous forms of life; the 20th discovered the world of minute ones.

The last few decades have witnessed the dawn of a new era. The most comprehensive of all the natural sciences, palaeontology makes use of techniques that range from field excavation to laboratory preparation and analysis (including chemicals, scanning electron microscopes and computers) to detect fossils and separate them from surrounding material. The study of ancient life has grown more efficient and is less apt to be romanticized. But palaeontologists keep picking away at the rock, hoping to add to the list of vanished species. They know they have barely scratched the surface.

The body of a mummified baby mammoth, preserved intact in the permafrost for 12,000 years, was found in Siberia in 1977. It was, however, only the latest in a series of such discoveries. The first mammoth skeleton ever to be retrieved was mounted in 1806. In 1901 the first scientific expedition to the region returned with a frozen mammoth that has been displayed in St Petersburg, Russia, ever since.

Overleaf: A fanciful 1886 engraving of a prehistoric creature.

DOCUMENTS

From yesterday's curiosity seekers
to today's palaeontologists

Strange fiction based on an even stranger past

French novelist Jules Verne is just one of many authors who have been intrigued by prehistory and have fabricated their own tales of palaeontological pursuits.

In his second major novel, Journey to the Centre of the Earth *(1864), Jules Verne (1828–1905) spins a fabulous tale of subterranean exploration that is full of poetry and visionary power yet rooted in the author's extensive knowledge of geology and palaeontology.*

Here, Axel and his uncle, Professor Lidenbrock, who together had discovered the existence of a secret passageway leading to the earth's centre, travel across a prehistoric sea thousands of miles beneath the earth's surface.

Maybe we will encounter some of those saurians that science has been able to reconstruct from bits of bone or cartilage.

I took the telescope and examined the sea. I saw nothing on its surface. We were probably still too near the shore.

I looked up in the air. Why shouldn't some of those birds reconstructed by the immortal Cuvier be flapping their wings in the heavy atmosphere? The fish would provide them with enough food. I scanned the space above me, but the air was as uninhabited as the shore.

My imagination, however, took me into the wonderful hypotheses of palaeontology. Dreaming with my eyes open, I seemed to see enormous prehistoric sea turtles moving across the water like floating islands. Along the darkened shore passed the great mammals of the earth's early times: the leptotherium, found in Brazilian caves, and the mericotherium, from the icy regions of Siberia. Farther on, the lophiodon, a giant tapir, was hiding

Jules Verne.

behind the rocks, ready to fight for its prey with the anoplotherium, a strange animal that looked like a mixture of rhinoceros, horse, hippopotamus and camel, as if the Creator, in too much of a hurry at the beginning of the world, had combined several animals in one. The giant mastodon waved its trunk and rammed its tusks against rocks on the shore, and the megathere, buttressed on its enormous legs, dug into the ground while its roars echoed loudly from granite cliffs. Higher up, the protopithecus, the first ape to appear on the surface of the globe, was climbing the steep peaks. Still higher, the pterodactyl, with its winged hands, was gliding through the dense air like a gigantic bat. And finally, highest of all, immense birds, more powerful than the cassowary and larger than the ostrich, spread their vast wings and flew up until their heads touched the granite vault above them.

Axel's dream: 'That whole fossil world was reborn in my imagination.'

That whole fossil world was reborn in my imagination. I went back to the biblical periods of creation, long before man came into being, when the incomplete earth was not yet ready for him. My dream then took me back before the appearance of living creatures. The mammals disappeared, then the birds, then the reptiles of the Palaeozoic, and finally the fishes, crustaceans, molluscs and articulata. The zoophytes of the transition period also vanished. All earthly life was concentrated in me, and my heart was the only one beating in the depopulated world! There were no more seasons, no more climates; the heat of the globe steadily increased and neutralized that of the sun. Plants grew to prodigious size. I passed like a shadow among arborescent ferns, stepping hesitantly on iridescent marl and mottled sandstone; I leaned against the trunks of huge conifers; I lay down in the shade of sphenophyllales, asterophyllites and lycopods a hundred feet high.

Centuries passed like days. I went back through the series of the earth's transformations. Plants disappeared; granite rocks lost their purity; solids turned into liquids under the action of more intense heat; water flowed on the surface of the globe; it boiled and evaporated; vapours enveloped the earth, which gradually turned into a white-hot gaseous mass as big and bright as the sun.

Jules Verne
Journey to the Centre of the Earth
1864

Gideon Mantell had just discovered the first dinosaurs when German botanist and palaeontologist Franz Unger (1800–76) drew these monstrous creatures. An early attempt at reconstructing vanished animal life, the fanciful composites pictured here reflect the 19th century's affinity for graphic detail.

Victorians and fossils in the modern novel

The 20th-century writer John Fowles recreates a whole 19th-century world around the passions of a young palaeontologist. The setting is Lyme Regis in Dorset, still famous for its fossils. A strange young woman often wanders by the sea, where Charles does his fossil-hunting.

Lyme is situated in the centre of one of the rare outcrops of a stone known as blue lias. To the mere landscape enthusiast this stone is not attractive. An exceedingly gloomy grey in colour, a petrified mud in texture, it is a good deal more forbidding than it is picturesque. It is also treacherous, since its strata are brittle and have a tendency to slide, with the consequence that this little stretch of twelve miles or so of blue lias coast has lost more land to the sea in the course of history than almost any other in England. But its highly fossiliferous nature and its mobility make it a Mecca for the British palaeontologist. These last hundred years or more the commonest animal on its shores has been man – wielding a geologist's hammer.

Charles had already visited what was perhaps the most famous shop in the Lyme of those days – the Old Fossil Shop, founded by the remarkable Mary Anning, a woman without formal education but with a genius for discovering good – and on many occasions then unclassified – specimens. She was the first person to see the bones of *Ichthyosaurus platyodon*; and one of the meanest disgraces of British palaeontology is that although many scientists of the day gratefully used her finds to establish their own reputation, not one native type bears the specific *anningii*. To this distinguished local memory Charles had paid his homage – and his cash, for various ammonites and *Isocrina* he coveted for the cabinets that walled his study in London. However, he had one disappointment, for he was at that time specializing in a branch of which the Old Fossil Shop had few examples for sale.

This was the echinoderm, or petrified sea-urchin. They are sometimes called tests (from the Latin *testa*, a tile or earthen pot); by Americans, sand-dollars. Tests vary in shape, though they are always perfectly symmetrical; and they share a pattern of delicately burred striations. Quite apart from their scientific value (a vertical series taken from Beachy Head in the early 1860s was one of the first practical confirmations of the theory of evolution) they are very beautiful little objects; and they have the added charm that they are always difficult to find. You may search for days and not come on one; and a morning in which you find two or three is indeed a morning to remember. Perhaps, as a man with time to fill, a born amateur, this is unconsciously what attracted Charles to them; he had scientific reasons, of course, and with fellow-hobbyists he would say indignantly that the *Echinodermia* had been 'shamefully neglected', a familiar justification for spending too much time in too small a field. But whatever his motives he had fixed his heart on tests.

Now tests do not come out of the blue lias, but out of the superimposed strata of flint; and the fossil-shop keeper had advised him that it was the area west of the town where he would do best to search, and not necessarily on the shore....

Personal extinction Charles was aware of – no Victorian could not be. But general extinction was as absent a concept from his mind that day as the smallest cloud from the sky above him; and even though, when he finally resumed his stockings and gaiters and boots, he soon held a very concrete example of it in his hand.

It was a very fine fragment of lias with ammonite impressions, exquisitely clear, microcosms of macrocosms, whirled galaxies that catherine-wheeled their way across ten inches of rock. Having duly inscribed a label with the date and place of finding, he once again hopscotched out of science – this time, into love. He determined to give it to Ernestina when he returned. It was pretty enough for her to like; and after all, very soon it would come back to him, with her. Even better, the increased weight on his back made it a labour, as well as a gift. Duty, agreeable conformity to the epoch's current, raised its stern head....

She delved into the pockets of her coat and presented him, one in each hand, two excellent *Micraster* tests. He climbed close enough to distinguish them for what they were. Then he looked up in surprise at her unsmiling face. He remembered – he had talked briefly of palaeontology, of the importance of sea-urchins....

'They were once marine shells?'

He hesitated, then pointed to the features of the better of the two tests: the mouth, the ambulacra, the anus. As he talked, and was listened to with a grave interest, his disapproval evaporated. The girl's appearance was strange; but her mind – as two or three questions she asked showed – was very far from deranged. Finally he put the two tests carefully in his own pocket.

'It is most kind of you to have looked for them.'

'I had nothing better to do.'

John Fowles
The French Lieutenant's Woman
1969

The observations of Leonardo da Vinci

Leonardo da Vinci (1452–1519), was the first to question the prevailing views on fossils, from the study of sedimentary rock layers. His notebooks were not deciphered until the 19th century, but he may have influenced others whose similar conclusions were published at the time.

Of the Deluge and of Marine Shells

In this work you have first to prove that the shells at a thousand braccia of elevation were not carried there by the deluge, because they are seen to be all at one level, and many mountains are seen to be above that level; and to inquire whether the deluge was caused by rain or by the swelling of the sea; and then you must show how, neither by rain nor by swelling of the rivers, nor by the overflow of this sea, could the shells – being heavy objects – be floated up the mountains by the sea, nor have [been] carried there by the rivers against the course of their waters....

All marine clays still contain shells, and the shells are petrified together with the clay. From their firmness and unity some persons will have it that these animals were carried up to places remote from the sea by the deluge. Another sect of ignorant persons declare that Nature or Heaven created them in these places by celestial influences, as if in these places we did not also find the bones of fishes which have taken a long time to grow; and as if we could not count, in the shells of cockles and snails, the years and

months of their life, as we do in the horns of bulls and oxen....

And if you were to say that these shells were created, and were continually being created in such places by the nature of the spot, and of the heavens which might have some influence there, such an opinion cannot exist in a brain of much reason; because here are the years of their growth, numbered on their shells, and there are large and small ones to be seen which could not have grown without food, and could not have fed without motion – and here they could not move....

As to those who say that shells existed for a long time and were born at a distance from the sea, from the nature of the place and of the cycles, which can influence a place to produce such creatures – to them it may be answered: such an influence could not place the animals all on one line, except those of the same sort and age; and not the old with the young, nor some with an operculum and others without their operculum, nor some broken and others whole, nor some filled with sea-sand and large and small fragments of other shells inside the whole shells which remained open; nor the claws of crabs without the rest of their bodies; nor the shells of other species stuck on to them like animals which have moved about on them; since the traces of their track still remain, on the outside, after the manner of worms in the wood which they ate into. Nor would there be found among them the bones and teeth of fish which some call arrows and others serpents' tongues, nor would so many portions of various animals be found all together if they had not been thrown on the sea shore.

Leonardo da Vinci,
The Notebooks of Leonardo da Vinci,
vol. I, compiled and
edited by Jean Paul Richter,
1970

Bernard Palissy: a passion for nature

Bernard Palissy (1510–89) was one of the great forerunners of modern palaeontology. A meticulous observer, he independently arrived at the same conclusions about fossils as Leonardo da Vinci. Palissy remained unsung until the 18th century, when Buffon and, later, Cuvier were among the first to give him his due. Palissy's writings were published in 1880.

During his lifetime Palissy was known not as a naturalist but as a skilled potter — for many years working under the patronage of members of the French aristocracy. All along, however, he lectured on natural history and was one of the first people to explain correctly the origin of fossils.

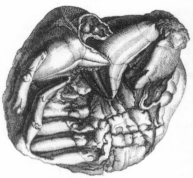

A portrait of Palissy (left) and a 17th-century engraving of a fossil crab (above).

That the mud and the shells have changed their nature by the same power and the same efficient cause I have proved before my hearers by showing them a large rock I had cut away from a cliff near Soubize, a city adjacent to the sea: The cliff was once covered by sea water, and before it turned to stone, there were a great many shellfish of several kinds which had died in the mud, and after the sea retreated from the spot, the mud and the fish were petrified. For there can be no doubt that the sea has retreated from there....

And because there are also rocks filled with shells, even on the summits of high mountains, you must not think that these shells were formed, as some

Albula Diluviana ex Landgraviatu Hassiæ in Lapid. fissili minus.

Lucius fossilis ex montibus Tripoli Syriæ vicinis.

Above: 17th-century engravings of fossil fish.

say, because Nature amuses itself with making something new. When I closely examined the shape of the rocks, I found that none of them can take the shape of a shell or other animal if the animal itself has not built its shape.... I have drawn a number of pictures of the petrified shells that can be found by the thousands in the Ardennes mountains [in northeastern France], and not just shells, but fish that have been petrified with their shells. And to show more clearly that the sea did not bring in these shells at the time of the Flood, ...

It must therefore be concluded that before these shells were petrified, the fish that made them lived in the water that had collected in these mountains and that since then the water and the fish were petrified at the same time, and of that you may be sure. In the Ardennes Mountains petrified mussels are found by the thousands, quite similar to those now living in the Meuse, which flows near these mountains.... I have always done my utmost to find more and more petrified things, and all told I have found more kinds of fish, or the shells thereof, petrified in the earth, than I have of modern kinds now living in the Ocean sea.

Bernard Palissy
'Of Stones'
Discours Admirables
(a collection of discourses)
1580

Precious tokens of antiquity

Robert Hooke (1635–1703), a leading British scientist of the 17th century, was the first to examine fossils with the compound microscope, to compare the internal structure of petrified wood with living wood and to relate ammonites to the living nautilus. His work is full of ideas and observations on geology and the history of life, many of which were to be taken up by later generations of scientists. He built up a 'repository' of fossils for the Royal Society, and advocated a central collection of natural history for scientific reference and study.

There have been many other species of creatures in former ages, of which we can find none at present; and 'tis not unlikely also but that there may be divers new kinds now, which have not been from the beginning....

There may have been divers new varieties generated of the same species, and that by the change of soil on which it was produced; for since we find that the alteration of the climate, soil and nourishment doth often produce a very great alteration in those bodies that suffer it; 'tis not to be doubted but that alterations also of this nature may cause a very great change in the shape, and other accidents of the animated body....; hence I suppose 'tis that I find divers kinds of petrify'd shells, of which kind we have none now naturally produced....

Now these shells and other bodies are the medals, urnes, or monuments of nature whose...impressions, forms, etc are...plain and discoverable to any unbiassed person, and therefore he has no reason...to desist from making his observations to correct his natural chronology.... These are the greatest and most lasting monuments of antiquity, which in all probability will far antedate all the most ancient monuments of the world.... Nor will there be wanting *Media* or *Criteria* of chronology....

Many, nay most, of them are of somewhat a differing shape, and of a much greater magnitude than are the shell-fishes of the like animals to be found upon the coast of Portland, or near the places where they have been found...

Consider whether it may not have been possible, that this very land of England and Portland did at a certain time for some ages past, lie within the torrid zone....

Many submarine regions must become dry land, and many other lands will be overflown by the sea, and these variations being slow, and by degrees will leave very lasting remarks of such states and positions, in the superficial substance of the earth....

I do...humbly conceive (tho' some possibly may think there is too much notice taken of such a trivial thing as a rotten shell, yet) that men do generally too much slight...these records of antiquity which nature have left as monuments and hieroglyphick characters of preceding transactions in the like duration...of the body of the earth, which are infinitely more evident and certain tokens than anything of antiquity that can be fetched out of coins or medals, or any other way yet known, since the best of those ways may be counterfeited or made by art and design... And tho' it must be granted, that it is very difficult to read them, and to raise a *Chronology* out of them, and to state the intervalls of the times wherein such, or such catastrophies and mutations have happened; yet 'tis not impossible but that, by the help of those joined to other means...of information, much may be done....

We will for the present take this supposition to be real and true, that there have been in former times of the world, divers species of creatures, that are now quite lost, and no more of them surviving upon any part of the earth. Again, that there are now divers species of creatures which never exceed at present a certain magnitude, which yet, in former ages of the world, were usually of a much greater and gygantick standard; suppose ten times as big as at present; we will grant also a supposition that several species may really not have been created of the very shapes they now are of, but that they have changed in great part their shape, as well as dwindled and degenerated into a dwarfish progeny; that this may have been so considerable, as that if we could have seen both together, we should not have judged them of the same species.... There may have been, by mixture of creatures, produced a sort differing in shape...from the true created shapes of both of them....

There is no impossibility in the supposition that every part[of the earth] hath, at some time or other, been shaken, overturned, or some way or other subject to earthquakes, and trans-formed by them.... One may easily believe that many changes may have happened to the earth, of which we can have no written history or accounts. And to me it seems very absurd to conclude, that from the beginning things have continued in the same state that we now find them, since we find everything to change and vary in our own rememberance; certainly 'tis a vain thing to make experiments and collect observations, if when we have them, we may not make use of them; if we must not believe our senses; if we may not judge of things by trials and sensible proofs, if we may not be allowed to make necessary consectaries and corollaries, but must remain tied up to the opinions we have received from others....

Robert Hooke
Discourse of Earthquakes from
The Posthumous Works of Robert Hooke
1705

The epochs of nature

On 5 August 1773, French naturalist Georges-Louis Leclerc de Buffon (1707–88) spoke on the epochs of nature to a group of scholars in Dijon. The text of his speech was printed five years later and denounced by the theology faculty of the University of Paris. In November 1779 Buffon, then seventy-two, left Dijon, to avert more serious consequences .

Much of Buffon's life was devoted to his monumental 44-volume Histoire Naturelle *(Natural History), published between 1749 and 1804.* Les Epoques de la Nature *(The Epochs of Nature), from which the excerpts below were taken, is one volume of this work.*

The age of the Earth

First Epoch, 'When the Earth and the planets were formed'

By comparing the heat of the planets and that of earth, we have seen that the incandescence of the terrestrial sphere lasted 2936 years; that for a period of 34,270 years it was so hot as to be untouchable; making a total of 37,206 years. That is the earliest point at which living nature could have come into existence.

The age of life

Third Epoch, 'When the continents were covered with water'

It would not be an overstatement to reckon that to bring about these mighty operations and tremendous formations nature required 20,000 years from the emergence of the first shellfish and first plants....

The continents were covered by water for a long time. To demonstrate the certainty of this, one need only consider the vast number of marine organisms which can be found down to fairly great depths and up to very considerable heights in all parts of the world. And should we not add to this already lengthy period the time it took for these marine organisms to be

Georges-Louis Leclerc de Buffon.

A s can be seen in this 1886 reconstruction of a primeval landscape, the earth was then
believed – at least by some – to have been convulsed by a succession of catastrophic events.

broken up, reduced to powder,
conveyed by the motion of the waters,
and subsequently to form marble,
limestone, and chalk? Indeed, this
long succession of centuries, this span
of 20,000 years, seems to me still too
brief a period for the sequence of events
that all of this activity suggests to us.

Before there was life on Earth

*Fourth Epoch, 'When the waters
retreated and the volcanoes
became active'*

Imagine what the earth must have
looked like... 45,000 or 60,000 years
from the time of its formation. Deep
pools, swift watercourses and swirling
eddies in all low-lying areas; almost
continuous earthquakes caused by the
subsidence of caves and by frequent
volcanic explosions both above ground
and under water; widespread and
local storms; whirlwinds of smoke,
windstorms whipped up by the
violent tremors in the earth and sea;
submersion and flooding; deluges
resulting from the aforementioned
disturbances; rivers of bitumen,
sulphur, and molten glass cutting a
swathe of destruction down the
mountains and on to flat open
country, poisoning the waters; the
sun itself almost continually obscured,
not only by aqueous clouds, but by
the thick pall of rock and ash ejected
by the volcanoes; and we give thanks
to the Creator for having spared man
the dreadful and terrifying sights that
preceded him and which, as it were,
heralded the birth of intelligent,
sentient nature.

Georges-Louis Leclerc de Buffon
The Epochs of Nature
1778

Cuvier's 'Catastrophism'

Georges Cuvier (1769–1832) believed that the catastrophes which convulsed the earth were not hypothetical but could be proved by observation of current phenomena. The 'inevitability of inter-ruptions in the chain of living things' was, he contended, a 'demonstrable certainty.' This view had its tenacious supporters, but its detractors were just as determined; and it was they who ultimately prevailed.

When the traveller passes over those fertile plains where the peaceful waters preserve, by their regular course, an abundant vegetation, and the soil of which, crowded by an extensive population, enriched by flourishing villages, vast cities, and splendid monuments, is never disturbed but by the ravages of war, or the oppression of despotism, he is not inclined to believe that nature has had her intestinal wars, and that the globe's surface has been overthrown by revolutions and catastophes. His opinions change, however, as he begins to penetrate into that soil, so peaceful now, or as he ascends the hills which bound the plain....

The traces of revolutions become more striking when we ascend higher, when we approach closer to the foot of the great chain of mountains.... Thus the sea, before the formation of horizontal layers, had formed others which had been broken up, formed again, again destroyed in a thousand ways. Therefore ... the sea ... underwent at least one catastrophe....

We must perceive that in the midst of such changes in the nature of the liquid, the animals which it nourished could not remain the same. The species, their very genus, changed with the layers....

But it is of great importance to note that these repeated irruptions and retreats have not all been gradual, not all uniform; on the contrary, the greater portion of these catastrophes have been sudden.... Existence has thus been often troubled on this earth by appalling events; calamities which, in the beginning, may have shaken to a considerable depth the entire envelope of the planet, but which have since become less deep and less widespread.

The Paris Museum of Natural History's Hall of Comparative Anatomy (above) and a portrait of Cuvier (opposite).

Living creatures without number have fallen victim to these catastrophes; some, the inhabitants of dry land, have been swallowed up by a deluge; others (who peopled the depths of the water) have been cast on land by the sudden receding of the waters, their very race become extinct, and only a few remains left of them in the world, scarcely recognized by the naturalist....

If there be anything determined in geology, it is that the surface of our globe has been subjected to a vast and sudden revolution, not further back than from five to six thousand years; that this revolution has buried and the countries formerly inhabited by man, and the species of animals now most known; that on the other hand it has left the bottom of the former sea dry, and has formed on it the countries now inhabited; that since the revolution, those few individuals whom it spared have been spread and propagated over the lands left newly dry, and consequently it is only since this epoch that our societies have assumed a progressive march, have formed establishments, raised monuments, collected natural facts and combined scientific systems....

Cuvier was careful to clarify the purported causes of these changes in animal life:

When I assert that the rocky beds contain the bones of various genera, and the shifting or alluvial strata those of many species which no longer exist, I do not mean to allege that a new creation was necessary to produce the species now existing; I only maintain that they did not exist in the place where we now see them, and they must have been deposited there by other means.

Georges Cuvier,
A Discourse on the Revolution of the Surface of the Globe, 1829

One of the founders of scientific palaeontology

William Smith (1769-1839) ranks with Cuvier and Lamarck in his contribution to palaeontology. As a canal engineer, he noticed that the different rock strata could be identified by the fossils he collected from them. In 1815 he published the first large-scale geological map, showing the strata of England and Wales.

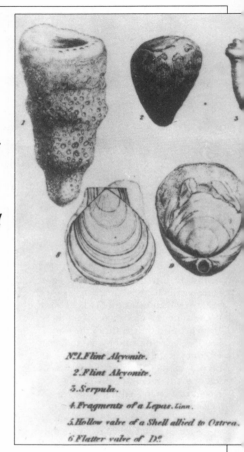

N.º 1. Flint Alcyonite.
2. Flint Alcyonite.
3. Serpula.
4. Fragments of a Lepas. Linn.
5. Hollow valve of a Shell allied to Ostrea.
6. Flatter valve of D.º

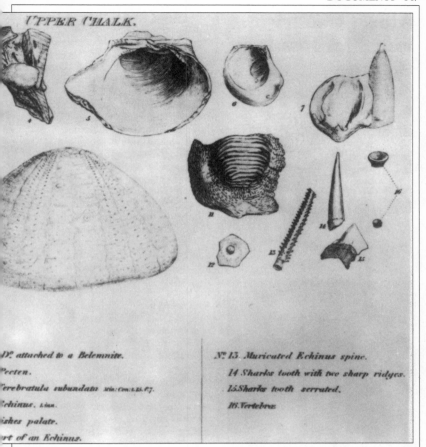

UPPER CHALK.

..ly. attached to a Belemnite.

..Pecten.

..erebratula subundata Min:Con:t.15.f.7.

..chinus. Linn.

..ishes palate.

..rt of an Echinus.

N° 13. Muricated Echinus spine.

14 Sharks tooth with two sharp ridges.

15.Sharks tooth serrated.

16.Vertebra.

Plate III of William Smith's *Strata Identified by Organized Fossils* published in 1816. It shows fossils from the stratum called Upper Chalk. Robert Hooke had suggested a century earlier that rocks might be dated by their fossils, but it was William Smith's work, and his realization that strata could be identified across continents, which helped to make possible the tremendous advances in geology in the 19th century.

Albert Gaudry hunts for fossils at Pikermi

Over a century ago, a young Frenchman named Albert Gaudry (1827–1908) made two discoveries: Greece and palaeontology. Through him, the fossil site at Pikermi would gain worldwide renown.

The Pikermi fossil site is located in Attica, a four-hour walk northeast from Athens and two hours from the Euboean Sea. You can get there via the new Marathon road.... You veer off the road to the right and head for Mt Pentelicus; a quarter of an hour later you reach a torrent that rushes down the mountainside. Some call it the Draphi,... others the Pikermi....

The countryside all around is exceedingly wild; in the distance, however, like everywhere else in Attica, magnificent vistas unfold before you.... These white, bare, marble mountains afford the traveller no shade, but the dazzling colours that play across them in the sunlight give them a beauty all their own.... The torrent is bordered by oleander, arbutus and here and there a tall tree. Exposed all along its deep, steeply sloping banks are hardened beds of red clay alternating with rolled pebbles. It is here, in these beds, that the fossil remains are concentrated....

I found myself hampered by the flows of water when I excavated here in the winter of 1855–6. In 1860, therefore, I resolved to dig during the hottest months of the year. The stream was a mere trickle and easily diverted; that was how I found my finest specimens. But working in such intense heat proved strenuous, and most of my men were stricken with malaria.

I pitched camp in the *metohi* [a cluster of huts] that was Pikermi. Someone had to be sent to Athens to obtain the bare necessities, even bread. I had brought along some camp beds. My own shelter was of a tent and a hut.

Albert Gaudry, left. Opposite: the countryside surrounding Athens.

The Greek Minister of War was kind enough to provide me with a protective escort of soldiers, and I cannot praise those splendid fellows highly enough. My previous excavation coincided with the days when bandits still roamed Greece.... We were constantly on the lookout but got off with only a few shots fired at us from out of range. By 1860, peace and quiet had been restored.

Our stay in camp was not entirely free from distress. There was the heat, the insects, the need to rise at daybreak and routinely forgo a siesta, the poor workers who had caught malaria while in my employ – all of those things cast an intermittent pall over the time we spent at Pikermi. And yet, now that I am back in our fair France, I have to confess that when I recall those Grecian sunbeams lighting the interior of my tent, that cloudless azure sky, the beautiful profile of those marble mountains, the Bay of Marathon glistening in the distance, I feel a little sad not to be at the foot of Mt Pentelicus!

Hours of misery would be followed by moments of delight. Time and again, our spirits were buoyed by the discovery of a hitherto unknown fossil.

If the day's efforts yielded an important find, we would have a little celebration come evening. There would be a goatskin bottle of retsina and some Hymettian honey; on occasion we even knocked some branches off an old pine tree and barbecued a sheep whole, palikar-style [soldier-style], the way they did it in Homer's time. Once we started to feel the wine, the workers, shepherds and soldiers would gather round the remnants of the fire and break into old Albanian songs; then a few of them would start dancing while others clapped hands to the rhythm. If a traveller roaming the foot of Mt Pentelicus had caught sight of our camp just then, he would have sworn we were a ring of fauns out of the days of Greek mythology.

Albert Gaudry,
The Geology and Fossil Animals of Attica,
1862–7

'Big Game' hunting in Canada

Barnum Brown (1873–1963) was a staff member of the American Museum of Natural History in New York City for sixty-six years, from 1897 until his death. A world-famous fossil hunter Barnum is particularly well known for his discovery of Tyrannosaurus rex in the Hell Creek region of Montana in 1902.

How and where collectors hunt Big Game of the past

Usually fossils are found in 'Bad Lands,' a name applied by the Jesuit missionaries to desolate regions denuded of grass and eroded into picturesque hills and ravines. In such places camp is located near some spring or stream, and the collectors ride or walk over the exposures till the region is thoroughly explored.

Quite different are the conditions on the Red Deer River. In places the canyon walls are nearly perpendicular, and the river winds in its narrow valley two to five hundred feet below the prairie, touching one side, then crossing to the other, so that it is impossible to follow up or down its course any great distance, even on horseback.

For many years the American Museum of Natural History of New York City has been making a systematic collection of fossils along this river, sending an expedition there every summer, and each succeeding expedition has returned with notable results. As the only feasible way to work these banks is from a boat, the parties proceed to the town of Red Deer, where the Calgary-Edmonton Railroad crosses the river.

There, with the aid of several carpenters, we constructed a flat-boat, 12 by 30 feet in dimension, similar to a Western ferry-boat. It was built upside down, and when caulked water-tight was turned over and launched in the river near by. This boat was capable of carrying ten tons with safety.

As the river has a speed of four miles per hour, we never intended to go upstream; so the boat was made on broad lines to be carried down by the current, its course directed by two great sweeps, or oars 22 feet long, one at each end of the boat, and nicely balanced on the gunwale, so that a man could push against it with his entire strength.

Supplied with a season's provisions, lumber for boxes, and plaster for encasing bones, we began our fossil cruise down a canyon that once echoed songs of the 'Bois Brûlé', for this river was at one time the home of many fur-bearing animals and within the Hudson Bay Company territory.

The first sixty miles of the river below the town of Red Deer is locally known as 'the Canyon', where the speed of the current is considerably more than four miles per hour, but there are alternating stretches of slow-moving water and rapids at low water dangerous to rafts and large boats.

Spruce and poplar trees cover this section of the country, and each bend of the river presents some picturesque vista of especial interest, the stately spruce trees, silhouetted against the sky, adding a charm to the ever-changing scene. Forest fires and lumbermen have thinned out most of the larger trees, and for miles along the river the underbrush was coloured pink by the ripe red raspberries.

In the long midsummer days, in latitude 52°, there are many hours of daylight, and constant floating would have carried us many miles per day; but frequent stops were made to prospect for fossils, and we rarely covered more than twenty miles per day. High up on the plateau buildings and haystacks proclaim a well-settled country, but habitations are rare along the river, and for miles we floated through picturesque solitude, the silence unbroken save by the noise of the rapids.

During the day an occasional flock of ducks or geese would be disturbed by our approach, though few signs of life were seen along the shore; but among the trees, when the mystic hush of night had stilled the camp, all the underworld was alive, and many little feet rustled the leaves where daylight disclosed no sign of life.

The night sounds of wild life

Then the muskrat and beaver would take courage to investigate the big intruder of their familiar haunts. From the distance some hungry coyote would send his plaintive cry echoing down the canyon, to be punctuated by the 'put-put-put, put, put' of a partridge drumming to his mate, and from the trees above came the constant query, 'Who-who – who-who-oo?'

At intervals we would tie up the boat and go ashore to search the banks, that fossils might not be overlooked. No large fossils were found in rocks of the Paskapoo age, but as soon as the Edmonton rocks appeared in the banks large bones of dinosaurs became numerous, and in the picturesque exposures at the mouth of Big Valley they were especially abundant.

Excavating with crooked awl and whisk-broom

At the foot of a butte lie scattered fragments of bone, and on the rivulet-scarred hillside other fragments appear, as we trace them up the waterways. Finally, ten, twenty or thirty feet above, other pieces protrude from the bank, and this is our lead. Cautiously we follow in from the exposed surface, uncovering the bone with crooked awl and whisk-broom, careful not to disturb the bone itself; for, although stone, it is usually checked and fractured in many places by former disturbance of its bed or crystallizing of mineral salts, and is rarely strong enough to permit removal.

Other bones may appear in the course of this preliminary work, and, if the find is desirable, the next step is carefully to gather every fragment, large and small, that has weathered out and fallen down the hillside; for when restored in the laboratory one of these pieces may be the critical point in the determination of a species.

Then with pick and shovel the heavy ledges above are removed, and often a team and scraper and dynamite are used when a large excavation is to be made. As we near the bone layer the work is more carefully done, with ever in mind the probable position of the bones of the skeleton. A false stroke of the pick in excavation may cause days of mending in the laboratory and might destroy some delicate bone.

When the bones are uncovered and brushed clean they are saturated with shellac till all small pieces adhere to each other; then the dirt is taken away from the sides, more shellac applied, and finally each bone stands on a little pedestal.

How the monster skeletons are packed

If the specimen is a skeleton, we next determine where the bones may be separated or broken to cause least damage, and each part is covered first with tissue paper, and then with two or three layers of plaster-of-Paris bandages – strips of burlap dipped in plaster. When this is set and thoroughly hard,

the block is undermined and turned over and bandages are applied to the lower surface to form a complete plaster jacket.

This preparation is slow and tedious. A skeleton may be uncovered in three days, but it will often take three weeks to prepare it ready for boxing. Then heavy boxes are made to dimension for each large block or several smaller ones, and the fossils are carefully packed in hay for shipment to the Museum.

Thus, at Tolman Ferry a few fragments which were seen protruding from a hillside developed into a complete skeleton. At first it was thought to be the well-known 'duck-bill' dinosaur Trachodon, but when the skull was revealed it was seen to be quite different. It proved to be related, but a form entirely new to science and since named Saurolophus, meaning crested saurian, from the long spine extending backward from the top of the head.

Zest in the hunt

Today there are thousands of different species of reptiles inhabiting the earth, and during each of the long prehistoric periods there were probably as many or more different kinds, for reptilian life is now on the wane.

Rarely does a season pass without several new genera being brought to light, and this possibility of discovery of the new and unknown adds zest to an already fascinating field of research. Any prospect may reveal some new creature of bizarre form, and we are constantly finding skeletons of animals known before by parts only.

The Edmonton formation has been especially interesting, for at least two-thirds of the species discovered in rocks of that age are new to science.

By the time we had reached Tolman, where a road crosses the river, our flat-boat, piled high with boxes of fossil animals, had become a veritable fossil ark. This was in the latter part of September; thin ice was forming on the river and it became too cold to do further effective collecting. The boat was then beached for the winter and the collection shipped back to the Museum.

Each summer work has been continued from the point at which it ceased the year before and the search has been carried on thoroughly.

Elsewhere complete dinosaur skeletons are rare, but in this part of Alberta they are not uncommon. In no other part of the world have so many Cretaceous dinosaur skeletons been brought to light. One American Museum expedition collected eight skeletons from a limited area exposed along three miles of the Red Deer River.

Camp life while on the hunt

Searching for prehistoric animals by boat is even more interesting than similar work in the arid 'Bad Lands' of the plains. Those who have husbanded drinking water on the desert through long hot summers keenly appreciate a river of snow water.

Pike, pickerel and sturgeon are caught in the Red Deer, and the persistent angler never fails to land a few 'gold-eyes', a species of fresh-water herring delicious when properly baked.

After a long day's search along the face of the hillsides or work in the quarry, the collector returns to camp hungry and exhausted, but soon to be revived by a good camp supper. Then the hour before sundown is spent with rod or motor-boat. The winds have ceased, and as the sun disappears over the rim, long purple shadows conjure fantastic forms on the rugged canyon walls; then a cheerful camp-fire, pipes and stories of other days and scenes.

All, of course, are not roseate scenes. The particular fly in our ointment has been the mosquitoes, which last year flocked to anything that moved, in numbers that I hesitate to estimate. But to the lover of camp life the days of discomfort and privation are those soonest forgotten.

As a result of the past four years' work in Canada, the American Museum expeditions have collected 300 large cases, or three and one-half carloads of fossils, two-thirds of which are exhibition specimens, including twenty skulls and fourteen skeletons of large dinosaurs, besides many partial skeletons. This material represents many genera and species new to science, and defines the anatomy and distribution of several heretofore but partially known creatures.

But the field has by no means been exhausted. Under miles of prairie land the same strata are undoubtedly filled with similar fossils; erosion is rapid, and as the river continues to wear its banks away new fossils are exposed. In a few years the same territory can be explored with similar results, and for all time to come the Red Deer River will be a classic locality for collecting prehistoric treasures.

Barnum Brown
'Hunting Big Game of Other Days'
National Geographic Magazine
vol. XXXV, no. 5, May 1919

Fossil evidence is still rewriting the history of life

New studies of the astonishing fossils of the Burgess Shale, discovered by Charles Walcott in 1909, suggest that ancient life was far more diverse than the creatures which have evolved from it, that survival is a lottery rather than a prize for the fittest.

Without hesitation or ambiguity, and fully mindful of such paleontological wonders as large dinosaurs and African ape-men, I state that the invertebrates of the Burgess Shale, found high in the Canadian Rockies in Yoho National Park, on the eastern border of British Columbia, are the world's most important animal fossils. Modern multicellular animals make their first uncontested appearance in the fossil record some 570 million years ago – and with a bang, not a protracted crescendo. This 'Cambrian explosion' marks the advent (at least into direct evidence) of virtually all major groups of modern animals – and all within the minuscule span, geologically speaking, of a few million years. The Burgess Shale represents a period just after this explosion, a time when the full range of its products inhabited our seas. These Canadian fossils are precious because they preserve in exquisite detail, down to the last filament of a trilobite's gill, or the components of a last meal in a worm's gut, the soft anatomy of organisms. Our fossil record is almost exclusively the story of hard parts. But most animals have none, and those that do often reveal very little about their anatomies in their outer coverings (what could you infer about a clam from its shell alone?). Hence, the rare soft-bodied faunas of the fossil record are precious windows into the true range and diversity of ancient life. The Burgess Shale is our only extensive, well-documented window upon that

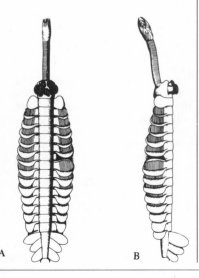

A   B

Whittington's reconstruction of *Opabinia*, a Burgess Shale creature. It has five eyes, a frontal nozzle, and paddle-shaped gills down each side of its body. Its anatomy does not match any known group.

most crucial event in the history of animal life, the first flowering of the Cambrian explosion....

In 1971, Professor Harry Whittington of Cambridge University published the first monograph in a comprehensive reexamination that began with Walcott's assumptions and ended with a radical interpretation not only for the Burgess Shale, but (by implication) for the entire history of life, including our own evolution....

Harry Whittington and his colleagues have shown...that the creatures from this single quarry in British Columbia probably exceed, in anatomical range, the entire spectrum of invertebrate life in today's oceans. Some fifteen to twenty Burgess species cannot be allied with any known group, and should probably be classified as separate phyla. Magnify some of them beyond the few centimeters of their actual size, and you are on the set of a science-fiction film....For species that can be classified within known phyla, Burgess anatomy far exceeds the modern range....Taxonomists have described almost a million species of arthropods, and all fit into four major groups; one quarry in British Columbia, representing the first explosion of multicellular life, reveals more than twenty additional arthropod designs! The history of life is a story of massive removal followed by differentiation within a few surviving stocks, not the conventional tale of steadily increasing excellence, complexity, and diversity....

So we return to Harry Whittington, facing the entire world's supply of *Opabinia*. Everyone had always identified this animal as an arthropod, but no one had found the smoking gun, the segmented appendages that define the group. But then, no one before Whittington had possessed the techniques needed to seek out small appendages hidden under an external carapace. A few years before, Harry had made the central methodological discovery that the Burgess Shale fossils are three-dimensional objects (however crushed), with top layers that one can dissect away, to reveal the structures underneath....

Opabinia virtually clamored for its crucial experiment under the new techniques: dissect through the carapace to find the body appendages and their attachments, dissect through the head shield to find the frontal appendages. So Harry dissected, in full confidence that he would find the jointed appendages of an arthropod. Harry dissected – *and he found nothing under the carapace.*

Opabinia was not an arthropod. And it sure as hell wasn't anything else that anyone could specify either....

I believe that Whittington's reconstruction of *Opabinia* in 1975 will stand as one of the great documents in the history of human knowledge. How many other empirical studies have led directly on to a fundamentally revised view about the history of life? We are awestruck by *Tyrannosaurus*; we marvel at the feathers of *Archaeopteryx*; we revel in every scrap of fossil human bone from Africa. But none of these has taught us anywhere near so much about the nature of evolution as a little two-inch Cambrian odd-ball invertebrate named *Opabinia*.

Stephen Jay Gould
Wonderful Life: The Burgess Shale and the Nature of History
1990

Matter, time, and fossilization

For centuries, fossilization was known simply as 'petrifaction'. Gradually, however, the intricacies of the making of a fossil came to be understood. The combination of biological, physical and chemical phenomena transforms dead organisms in a way that preserves their features for all time.

Silicified trunk of a willow tree from the Cenozoic (35 million years ago). The growth rings and tissue patterns of spring and autumn are clearly visible.

What is a fossil?

A dead organism becomes a fossil when the spaces once filled by its organic matter are replaced by mineral substances. It literally turns to stone – but only under special conditions.

First prerequisite: the dead organism must be quickly buried in the sand, mud or ooze so that it will not disintegrate. One favourable environment is the bottom of a sea or lake. Consequently, fossils of marine organisms are far more abundant and far better preserved than those of land organisms (although conditions in steppes and deserts are also conducive to fossil formation).

Secondly, there must be no (or very little) decomposition; instead, there must be gradual replacement of organic matter by mineral substances.

Thirdly, for a fossil to survive whole for millions of years, it cannot be subjected to folding, heat buildup in the earth's interior, or other potentially destructive disturbances. Fossil-bearing strata are therefore more apt to be found in calm sedementary basins than in geologically active mountainous regions.

What becomes of living things?

A complex process of decomposition peculiar to vegetable matter turns plants into lignite, a form of coal. Occasionally leaves and stems leave only mineralized impressions in the rock. Some tree trunks will completely silicify. Pine-tree resin is transformed into amber.

Usually all that remains of animals is their internal or external supporting structure: the tests [a hard external covering] of microorganisms, the skeletal material of corals, shellfish valves, arthropod carapaces [a bony shield covering an animal's back], the thecae [an enveloping sheath] of echinoderms, fish scales, vertebrate bones and teeth, and eggshells.

An original mineral substance (calcium carbonate or silica) can be preserved, or replaced, by any number of substances, including silica, gypsum, pyrite, marcasite, hematite and bitumen.

Cellulose can be preserved as plant spores or as microfossils trapped inside the flint nodules that form in chalk.

Extremely delicate body parts – insect antennae, feet, wings, bird feathers, flower stamens – have been known to survive intact.

Perfectly preserved fine structures – magnified up to 80,000 times – are visible under the scanning electron microscope: the nacreous [like mother-of-pearl] tissue of shellfish, the cellular matter of plants, the sculptured surfaces of pollen grains, the tubercules of tiny teeth and the microstructure of corals.

Are soft body parts also preserved?

Preservation of soft body parts has been known to occur, but only very rarely. In some cases, all that remains of a once-extant fossil is an impression. Other fossils can be destroyed in a way that preserves their internal tissue, but nothing else.

Coprolites, the fossilized faeces of vertebrates are clues to an animal's feeding activity and can tell us whether it was a meat-eater or a plant-eater. At some sites, tracks, trails and footprints are relatively abundant.

An extreme case of preservation are the woolly mammoths and rhinoceroses, frozen solid in the permafrost of Siberia for tens of thousands of years. These genuinely 'flesh-and-bone' fossils are very fragile and decompose when exposed to above-ground conditions.

Yvette Gayrard-Valy

A frog from the Oligocene (35 million years ago), 'mummified' in calcium phosphate.

Cross section of *Conoceras,* a fossil nautilus from the Jurassic (170 million years ago).

The delicate forms of *Diploastrea,* a reef-building coral from the Miocene (15 million years ago) of Landes, a region of southwestern France that once was covered by a tropical sea.

A blossom of Bennettitales, a fossil plant from the Jurassic (170 million years ago).

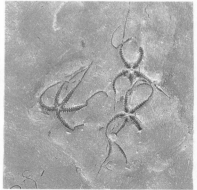

Fossil brittle stars preserved in mud from the Devonian (380 million years ago).

An extremely rare specimen of the Jurassic sea urchin *Pseudocidaris* (150 million years ago) with its long, thick spines still attached.

A beautifully preserved fossil of the Triassic shrimp *Aeger* (210 million years ago) from the lithographic limestone of Solnhofen, in western Germany.

Seed-fern frond from the Carboniferous (320 million years ago).

Bird feathers from the Oligocene (30 million years ago) of central France.

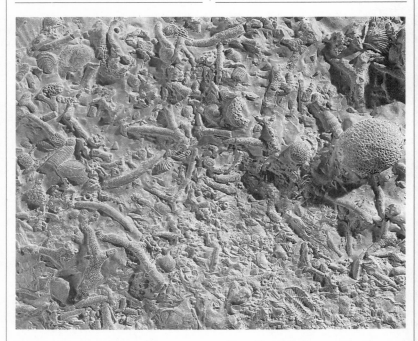

Preservation of even the most delicate structures and branchings makes it easy to identify the invertebrates embedded in this fossil-rich limestone from the Silurian (415 million years ago) of Dudley, England.

This poplar leaf from the Miocene of Germany is 20 million years old. All of its veins and part of its cuticle are clearly visible.

Traces in the Stone

Unquestionably the most thrilling evidence of past life, fossil footprints and other fossil vestiges are fragile, intimate traces of biological activity that have been miraculously preserved. Research into this phenomenon blossomed into a fully-fledged discipline known as palaeoichnology.

People began to notice fossil footprints, especially those made by dinosaurs or other large vertebrates, a very long time ago. They were slow to acknowledge their true identity, and for hundreds of years the tracks were attributed to human giants from before the Flood. In time, less spectacular trace fossils left by smaller animals, such as salamanders, came to light: tail or belly trails, burrows and tunnels, tubular dwelling structures hollowed out by molluscs, clusters of eggs, telltale signs of feeding activity, various holes and perforations, grooves left by worms, and the delicately furrowed traces of arthropod legs.

How did they come to be preserved? First, the ground had to be soft (thus, trace fossils can also provide clues about vanished shorelines and swamps and show how deep the water may have been). Next, the mud through which the animal moved had to dry and harden before being covered by another layer. Finally, the sediment had to be spared any geological disturbance. After transforming into rock, shale, marl or sandstone, the two layers had to remain separate so that on removal they would break apart cleanly and expose the

It was once thought that fossil footprints, like the ones in these 19th-century drawings, were left by animals that lived before the Flood.

Footprints of a large, four-legged herbivorous dinosaur preserved in western Morocco in rock that was once Cretaceous ooze.

impression. Animal tracks can be preserved as natural moulds or casts (hollow or raised, respectively). Curiously, a site rich in animal tracks, may yield very few fossil bones.

As one studies and interprets trace fossils, intuition and even imagination take over where methodical analysis leaves off. An animal can leave behind very different traces depending on whether it was plodding along, running or jumping at the time. A tailed amphibian, such as a salamander or newt, can walk along the edge of a marsh, swim through it, or touch the bottom. To interpret these types of fossils they must be compared with traces left by living forms. Animals believed to be relatively similar are closely observed as they move across, say, fresh plaster or soft clay.

Drawing conclusions about the exact identity of an animal that left its mark tens or even hundreds of millions of years ago is easier said than done. (Some trace fossils date all the way back to the Paleozoic, about 300 million years ago.) In some instances several tracks intersect and merge, suggesting concentrated animal activity.

Even when it is all but impossible to pinpoint species, a trace fossil can prove helpful in determining the classificatory group an animal may have belonged to (for example, certain dinosaur families and not others). It can give us a rough idea of the animal's size, shape, weight and general appearance. A trace fossil can also provide clues about the original composition and depth of the animal's sedimentary environment and about the possible location of prehistoric shorelines.

Scientists use these fragile, elusive imprints to corroborate and augment the precise, systematic research that is conducted on more dependable types of fossils. Sound reconstructions of vanished worlds depend upon the scientists' ability to decipher these fossil records.

Yvette Gayrard-Valy

In the coal forests

There is something uncanny about the vast primeval forests that subsided into the earth during the Carboniferous period (345 to 280 million years ago) to form the world's coal deposits.

Reconstructions of primeval plant life often to their imagination.

Fossil impressions of carboniferous ferns are found in shale deposits between coal layers.

The Carboniferous is the best known and one of the most important of all fossil-bearing geological periods. Nurtured by a rainy climate, the marshy forests then in existence sheltered lush vegetation that carpeted

feature the well-known flora of the coal forests, a magical world in which illustrators give free rein

vast expanses of what is now Europe and large stretches of eastern North America.

The giant of the landscape was the lycopod, or club moss, Lepidodendron (from *'lepid'*, meaning scale – named after the characteristic leaf scars on its outer cortex). Its thick roots twisted up from the ooze into huge columnar trunks a yard across that soared over 40 metres straight into the air and ended in a broad, umbrella-like crown of leaves. Another large tree, Sigillaria (also a lycopod), sprouted clumps of long, grasslike leaves nearly 30 metres above the forest floor.

This majestic stand of growth was dense with calamites, huge horsetail-like species with massive jointed stems reaching nearly 10 metres in height. With their fine, tapered leaves, calamites resembled modern bamboo.

Another Carboniferous plant group was Cordaitales, an arborescent order of plants similar in habit to the araucaria family of coniferous trees. The slender stems of these plants, which grew from 30 to 40 metres tall, were capped by long, strap-shaped leaves.

The tree ferns, best known of all of this strange flora, had true roots, stems, and leaves. Their broad fronds emerged from rather slender stems that rose 10 metres or so into the air. A thick pad of fallen fronds carpeted the base of the central stem.

Not all ferns were true ferns. Many species were pteridosperms, or 'seed ferns,' with strongly denticulate, or serrated, leaves that are deceptively fernlike. Now totally extinct, these plants grew 3 or 4 metres tall and resembled small trees or shrubs; their trunks measured up to 50 centimetres in diameter.

This tangle of luxuriant growth wove a suffocating web of vegetation. Trunks took root in a spongy forest floor that often gave way to vast expanses of swamp. The place literally crawled with creatures: countless spiders, 50-centimetre-long millipedes, and insects of every description. There were swarms of cockroaches, and giant dragonflies with wingspans of over 70 centimetres buzzed through the sultry air.

Creatures of another sort crept along the swamps' edges. These were the amphibians, the first vertebrates with the ability to breathe out of water, tread dry land on four legs and utter sounds. They had big, heavy, bony skulls and were thus named stegocephalians ('roof-headed'). Extremely abundant in all parts of the world, they left countless footprints in the mud, just waiting to be discovered – 300 million years later!

Endless expanses of lush vegetation, odd-looking 19th century, when this geological period

What became of these mighty forests?

The ground beneath the forests was unstable. Slowly but surely, the supporting landmass became submerged. Whole forests settled into the ooze over a period of millions of years. The trees' roots, enormous trunks and magnificent leaves were fossilized into the treasure trove of amazingly well-preserved specimens so familiar to fossil enthusiasts today.

A good deal of the forests' vegetable matter underwent extensive decomposition and then fermented in the stagnant water. Transforming beyond recognition, the mulch first was compressed into peat and eventually hardened into coal in a process known as carbonization.

Yvette Gayrard-Valy

plants, stagnant swamps – such was the Carboniferous as it was reconstructed time and again in the typified what the earth presumably looked like before the Flood.

Fossils: servants of industry

Whatever the reason — their chemical composition or other special properties — fossils play a major part in detecting and tapping our planet's natural resources.

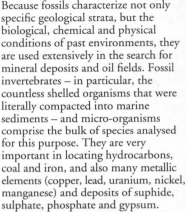

Because fossils characterize not only specific geological strata, but the biological, chemical and physical conditions of past environments, they are used extensively in the search for mineral deposits and oil fields. Fossil invertebrates – in particular, the countless shelled organisms that were literally compacted into marine sediments – and micro-organisms comprise the bulk of species analysed for this purpose. They are very important in locating hydrocarbons, coal and iron, and also many metallic elements (copper, lead, uranium, nickel, manganese) and deposits of suphide, sulphate, phosphate and gypsum.

Star fossils of modern geology, the foraminifera (large, mainly marine unicellular organisms) provide clues that can help pinpoint likely crude oil deposits. Organic matter in fossil form, oil is liquid rock created by the buildup of decomposed and consolidated organic matter into vast accumulations of microscopic plants (algae, spores, pollen) and marine micro-organisms.

Accumulations of living things also formed an extraordinarily diverse range of rocks that are utilized according to their characteristic properties.

The first mineral energy source to be tapped was coal, which is vegetable matter that first decomposed and then fossilized. Oil is the pre-eminent energy source of modern times. Both coal and oil are stored fossil fuels.

Carbonates, though less spectacular, are just as indispensable. Chalk, a calcium carbonate, has a great many industrial applications: in paints and putties, as an abrasive, a building stone

A derrick in an oil field.

(the white chateaux of the Loire valley are made of calcareous tufa, or travertine), a medium for prehistoric rock carvings, a source of lime, and an ingredient in cement and mortar. Limestone, similar to although harder than chalk, is quarried extensively for use as building stone in rubble or ashlar masonry and in monuments (as in the cities of Paris and Bath, for example).

Phosphorus derived from organic matter – either directly from shells and bones or indirectly through the decomposition of organic matter and excrement – is of tremendous importance in the chemical industry. Phosphates are used in everything from detergents and photographic products to fertilizers and pesticides.

Diatomite, a hard, lightweight, porous substance built up from accumulated diatom shells (diatoms are minute planktonic algae), is used as a filter in the production of sugar, pharmaceuticals and chemicals, as an absorbant in the production of dynamite, and as an ultrafine abrasive known as tripoli.

A less familiar example of biogenic siliceous rock is flint, which forms when the silica secreted by radiolarians (usually spherical marine protozoans), diatoms and sponges dissolves upon their death and is reprecipitated in crystalline form. The oldest substance to be used by primitive peoples and for tens of thousands of years the sole implement of human industry, flint was subsequently used in tinderboxes, flintlock firearms and road maintenance. The chief ingredient of concrete, it is a mainstay of modern construction.

Yvette Gayrard-Valy

Quarried since Roman times, the layers of sedimentary rock beneath Paris and its environs yielded the rubble and hewn stone used to build most of the city's houses and monuments.

The wondrous world of micropalaeontology

Micropalaeontology, the science of minute fossilized organisms, transports us into an extraordinary world of undreamed-of phenomena. Fossilization can preserve intact structures that must be magnified as much as 80,000 times under a scanning electron microscope before they can be examined.

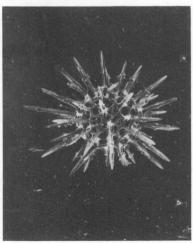

The world of minute life forms is extremely rich and diverse. Some of these microorganisms belong to the animal kingdom, others to the plant kingdom. They are the principal constituents of the world's plankton. Each consists of a single cell that secretes its own calcareous or siliceous exoskeleton, a shell-like protective coating, which is all that survives after the death of the organism. Countless numbers of these microscopic skeletons piled up over hundreds of millions of years, eventually forming massive layers of sediment.

Radiolaria are protozoans and therefore belong to the animal kingdom. They have been distributed in all parts of the world since Palaeozoic times. After the death of individual radiolarians, their hard, siliceous skeletons drop to the seafloor, where they accumulate over time and form rocks known as radiolarites.

Tens of thousands of radiolarian species have been identified. Their sculptured exoskeletons can take on a seemingly endless variety of shapes (helmets, footed urns, baskets, lanterns) and ornamentation (nested spheres, prisms with ornate spurs or spines).

Radiolarite is a hard, exceedingly fine-grained substance that polishes beautifully. Often found in mountain chains (including the Alps) in layers as much as hundreds of yards thick, this variety of cryptocrystalline quartz – commonly known as chalcedony – occurs in a wide range of beautiful colours, from lavender blue through every shade of violet, green and yellow imaginable to brick red and brown

A radiolarian viewed through a scanning electron microscope.

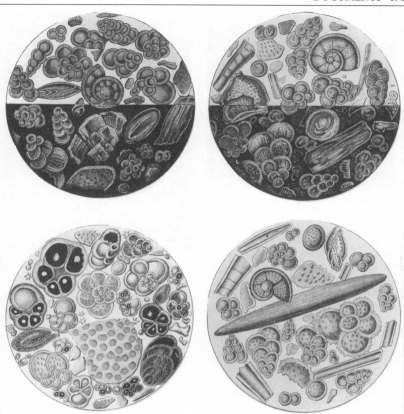

Nineteeth-century drawings of microfossils.

(jasper, agate, onyx and carnelian are all varieties of chalcedony). Prized as a gemstone since ancient times, it was chosen for such famous monuments as the Medici Chapel in Florence and the grand staircase in the Paris opera house and is still used in the making of statues, decorative objects and jewelry.

Another group of organisms with siliceous microskeletons, the diatoms, are algae that live in fresh and salt water. The oldest date from Mesozoic times, 100 to 250 million years ago. Each diatom secretes a frustule, a bivalve shell with intricately sculptured patterns. An endless variety of ornamentation – beads, lattices, spikes, spurs, rods, ribs, parallel or radiating

All images on this page and the page opposite were photographed using a scanning electron microsope.

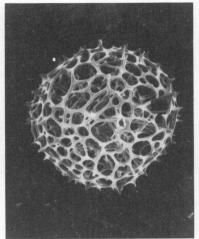

Two foraminiferans (left and directly above) and a radiolarian (top) from the Quaternary.

stripes – give them a truly jewel-like appearance. Countless diatom frustules collected in the ooze and eventually formed a substance called diatomaceous earth. An estimated 500 million diatoms are packed into a cubic metre of diatomite!

Like cryptocrystalline quartz, occurring as deposits up to hundreds of metres thick, this white, soft, generally crumbly substance is used as an abrasive (tripoli) and as a lightweight building stone. (The dome of Hagia Sophia in Istanbul, Turkey, is made entirely of diatomaceous material.)

Other unicellular algae, the coccolithophorids, were instrumental in the formation of another familiar sedimentary rock, chalk. Abundant in temperate and warm waters, the living organisms are encased in variously shaped calcareous shells known as coccoliths. They proliferated at an explosive rate during the Cretaceous period, the latter half of the Mesozoic era: It was during that period that chalk was laid down over virtually the whole of Europe. There are an estimated ten million coccoliths per cubic millimetre of chalk! The disproportion between the size of these minute marine organisms and the huge deposits they eventually formed is no less mind-boggling than the time that was needed to build up such vast quantities of fine calcareous ooze. In optimum conditions, a cubic metre of chalk contains the same number of coccolithophorids as 100,000 cubic metres of sea water.

Foraminifera are single-celled

T wo microscopic algae, or diatoms (above and left above), from the Quaternary.

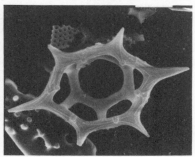

A radiolarian from the Quaternary.

animals with a usually calcareous shell, or test, which forms through the successive accretion of tiny, intricately structured chambers. That accounts in part for the organisms' astonishing diversity. In addition, their size varies from minuscule (one hundredth of a centimetre) to giants ten thousand times bigger (10 centimetres long)! Distributed in all parts of the world from the Palaeozoic to the present day, they, too, are important rock-builders.

In ancient times, a number of the larger and more oddly shaped foraminiferans were believed to be grains of wheat, coins or lentils, and inspired many legends.

Micropalaeontology has shed light on another intriguing phenomenon: the presence of non-mineralized planktonic microorganisms within flint nodules in chalk. As biogenic silica dissolved and was slowly reprecipitated in crystalline form – the exact process is not yet fully understood – these nodules trapped and literally mummified the tiny creatures, leaving their organic matter transformed but undisturbed and visible for all time.

Micropalaeontologists have studied many other microscopic groups too numerous to discuss here. However, spores and pollen, which are extremely abundant in certain sediments, cannot go unmentioned. Once identified, these minute grains can be used to reconstruct ancient floras, from them the environments of major geological periods, and from them the succession of sometimes unforeseen climates that have shaped life on our planet over millions of years.

Yvette Gayrard-Valy

The tasks and tools of palaeontology

Of all the disciplines associated with the natural sciences, palaeontology probably requires the widest range of scientific and technical expertise. Palaeontological research starts in the field and culminates in laboratory analysis.

Since palaeontologists have to probe the earth to get at their material, the first demand their profession makes upon them is the ability to do field work. Palaeontologists 'prospect' and dig, drawing on the expertise of geologists. As well as relying on their combined technical abilities, the members of the excavation team must also depend on a certain amount of drive and physical stamina.

Field techniques

Discoveries in the field can be a matter of luck: Any excavation by humans has the potential to unearth fossil remains. They also might be found protruding from an exposed cliff face, or, in desert regions, lying on ground that has been weathered away by atmospheric agents. However, chance discoveries are strictly hit-or-miss. To increase the odds of a find, palaeontologists begin by gathering all available geological data about a given area and assessing its potential for preserving organisms. Then a team of geologists, sedimentologists and palaeontologists conducts a systematic search and survey. It may take several excursions to pinpoint one or more likely dig sites.

Many of the various excavation techniques require elaborate equipment and strict field regimens; which technique is used depends on the nature of the fossils and of the sediments in which they are embedded. Once a fossil specimen is retrieved, it is sent to the laboratory, where it goes through certain procedures that will prepare it for study.

Palaeontologists working on a site in southern Morocco (left) and reconstructing a dinosaur skeleton (opposite).

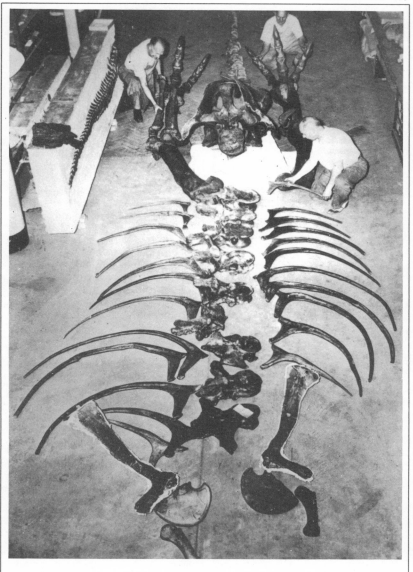

A laboratory worker using specially designed precision tools to clean away rock from a large jaw.

Preparation of specimens

A fossil may be difficult to handle because it is either fragile or already broken. Moreover, it will almost invariably be caked with sediment.

Larger specimens are removed from their rock matrices in the laboratory. If they have been encased in plaster for transport, their protective jacket must first be removed. Knives, scrapers and steel chisels are then used to clean the matrix away from the fossil.

When the surrounding slab is thin and the specimen small, technicians resort to steel needles, electric drills, tiny diamond-tipped saws or precision pneumatic picks. These procedures demand patience, manual dexterity and a thorough understanding of the specimen. Optical devices, such as hand lenses or binocular magnifying glasses, are almost always required.

Small sandblasters or ultrasonic tanks are used to extract very delicate impressions, such as scale patterns or bony dermal plates. Carbonate matrices are etched away with acid, provided the fossil is more acid-resistant than the rock around it. Safety precautions must be taken with this method, which usually calls for acetic acid or formic acid.

A fossil bone itself might be picked away if removing it promises to reveal the natural moulds of especially interesting anatomical spaces, such as the brain, nerves or blood vessels. Layers of a very thin solution of acetone glue are applied to harden the fossil as it emerges from the rock.

Flowers, leaves and minute skeletons must be embedded in polyester resin before they can be handled and studied. Viewing the internal morphology of these and other fragile structures requires highly specialized techniques. In series sectioning, for example, the fossil is microtomed, or sliced, into sections 20 microns thick. Series polishing – at intervals of 20 to 40 microns – is a variation on this procedure – except that it literally polishes the specimen away.

The fine internal structure of coelenterates and plants requires the preparation of sections 30 microns thick. Microscopic structures can be studied in ultra-thin sections polished down to a thickness of 2 microns, the threshold of unaided human vision. All thin sections are examined with a binocular loupe or under the microscope in normal or polarized light.

The individual teeth of minute mammals can be glued to the tips of needles that are then mounted on pieces of cork. If handling the originals is too risky, tiny resin casts are prepared for study under the scanning electron microscope.

Microfossils and plants

Sediment is ground away from microfossils (either fragments of larger fossils or entire microscopic organisms) and, if need be, etched away with acid or separated by flotation, which causes specimens to rise to the surface of a specially prepared fluid.

The same procedures are used for pollen and spores. Given the extreme thinness of leaf, rib, and stem impressions, the preparation of fossil plants requires highly specialized techniques.

Laboratory analysis

The following techniques involve specimen analysis and are specifically confined to the laboratory.

The most elementary procedure, direct observation, can yield much information about a fossil's size, colour, composition, state of preservation and matrix. Palaeontologists must bring all their expertise to bear and visually register as much detail as possible. A gift for observation is imperative.

Optical devices such as hand lenses and microscopes are essential, and optical fibres may be needed to probe interior spaces. The scanning electron microscope is indispensable for examining ultrafine external detail and microorganisms. Some fossil structures are so well preserved they can be magnified up to 80,000 times!

Since photographs must be taken at all stages of fossil preparation, palaeontological laboratories need to have all the necessary equipment to make and process black-and-white and colour exposures, photomacrographs, photomicrographs and stereophotographs using different kinds of light, including ultra-violet and infra-red.

Radiography is commonly used to locate a fossil inside its matrix. This technique can also reveal the details of a specimen's internal morphology, such as anatomical cavities and dental roots.

A fossil also has to be drawn. This requires a series of meticulous measurements – an indispensable stage of analysis in any event – which are then used to compare it with identical or closely related forms. A drawing can simplify, emphasize an important detail, enhance relief, or reconstruct missing parts.

Fossil analysis often involves the preparation of moulds and casts. If the specimen in question is an impression (an 'external mould'), the organism's original form can be restored by means of a substance that will harden once poured into the natural mould.

Lab work requires a delicate touch.

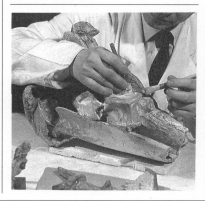

Moulding materials should be strong, highly dependable, easy to handle and versatile. Synthetic resin, latex rubber or dental modelling material is used for special casts; plaster of Paris is preferred for reconstructing damaged or missing parts and replicating a fossil specimen in its entirety.

Micro-organisms

The world of micro-organisms requires highly specialized physico-chemical techniques: examination under the microscope in polarized light, the use of ultraviolet light, scanning electron microscopy and electronic microanalysis.

Mathematical analysis

Modern palaeontology now relies on mathematics as never before. Using biometrics (statistical analysis of biological observations and phenomena), a palaeontologist can apply elementary statistical methods to sets of measurements that are selected according to the type of analysis desired. Computer-generated three-dimensional models are now an integral part of fossil analysis.

The palaeontologist of today

Those are the methods at modern palaeontology's command, the techniques palaeontologists of today can expect to use. Another, more subtle tool – scientific expertise – also comes into play. Given the staggering array of organisms spanning over 3500

million years, the need to specialize becomes obvious. A researcher might be a micropalaeontologist or an expert in vertebrates, often with a special interest in a specific group. In the field of palaeontology there are people who concentrate on foraminifers, bivalves, echinoderms, reptiles and microscopic mammals. Furthermore, each of

Discovery of a dinosaur skeleton in Niger. Weathering eroded the Cretaceous sediment, leaving the fossil exposed on the surface. The animal's spinal column is clearly visible.

these groups evolves over time, so a scientist's focus might further narrow to, say, the flora of the Carboniferous, Permotriassic amphibians, dinosaurs or the Equidae of the Pliocene.

Since palaeontologists start their research in the field, they must have a good grounding in geology, which is but one of the many disciplines they need if they are to understand and reconstruct the bewildering world of past life. The scope of their general knowledge must take in all of the natural sciences. Reconstructing vanished life-forms sheds light on their environment and living conditions, which in turn tie in with the gamut of natural phenomena over geological time – changes in the earth's atmosphere, the evolving configuration of landmasses and oceans and changes in climate.

Palaeontologists must also be conversant with the biological sciences – including elementary genetics and embryology – and biology's potential applications... to which list we should add the rudiments of physics, chemistry and mathematics.

Lastly, palaeontologists rely on bibliographical documentation to keep abreast of developments in their field. Before a discovery can be officially recognized it must be published. Thus, like scientists in other fields, palaeontologists are expected to report regularly on their findings, and to do so as clearly and as concisely as possible.

The palaeontologists of today no longer work in a vacuum. They are part of an interdisciplinary endeavour that draws on the combined abilities of researchers and technicians of all nationalities. To realize its full potential, modern palaeontology – the most multifaceted of all the natural sciences – must be a team effort in every way.

Yvette Gayrard-Valy
'Sur les Pas des Dinosaures'
(On the Trail of the Dinosaurs)
La Recherche, No. 102
February 1986

The role of palaeontology

Encompassing aspects of both the earth and life sciences, palaeontology draws on the expertise of specialists in both disciplines. In return it provides vital information and crucial supporting evidence for these scientists' theories. It is closely intertwined with all the natural sciences.

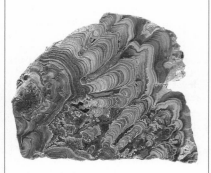

Stromatolite built up by single-celled algae during the Precambrian (2500 million years ago). In the Sahara desert region of Africa, stromatolites cover tens of square kilometeres.

Measuring geological time

It took the human mind hundreds of years to grasp the true nature of geological time. Fossils played a key part in this process once they finally assumed their proper place in the history of the earth. In 1830 Charles Lyell established the connection between the age of sedimentary rock layers and the fossils embedded within them. Some species were found to occur only in particular strata; these so-called index fossils serve as guides in the relative dating of sometimes widely separated deposits. Those containing the same fossils are the same age. Furthermore, the sequential arrangement of various fossils made it possible to reconstruct the chronological order in which sediments were laid down.

All of this led to the creation of an international stratigraphic time scale based primarily on the occurrence of index fossils in sediments. Developed a century ago, this relative chronology can be applied anywhere in the world.

Calculating the absolute date of strata in thousands or millions of years requires special analytical techniques, such as measuring the rate of disintegration of radioactive chemical elements in the earth – the ones that minerals and fossils are made of. Based on radiometric dating, it is estimated that the Palaeozoic era began 600 million years ago and that life first appeared 3800 million years ago!

Reconstructing prehistoric habitats

Geologists working in the field turn up all sorts of clues that they then use to identify depositional environments (continental, marine, folded, etc.) and determine how they formed. Close

A close relative of ammonites that lived only in Mesozoic times, the nautilus has survived for millions of years virtually unchanged. It is a 'living fossil.' The individual in this drawing from the 19th century is shown upside down. The animal uses its tentacles to propel itself through the water; the coiled body chamber should be on top.

examination of specimens prior to extraction yields valuable information about their original habitat and how they lived, died, accumulated and fossilized. In the laboratory, fossils can even tell us about such things as changes in climate, or the temperature, salinity, depth and chemical composition of an original marine environment. Entire prehistoric landscapes can be reconstructed from spores, pollen grains and other plant remains.

Confirming continental drift

When German geophysicist and meteorologist Alfred Wegener (1880–1930) put forth his famous theory of continental drift in 1912, he cited as evidence the way the continents seemed to fit together like pieces of a jigsaw puzzle, certain other geological phenomena and the fact that identical fossil plants and vertebrates had been discovered on widely separated continents. Since then, modern plate tectonics theory, which holds that the continents are embedded in plates that move about like drifting rafts on the earth's surface, has gained wide acceptance. Observation of fossil floras and faunas allowed scientists to chart the episodes of this geological process. Identical fossils on two continents? The land masses in question were once joined. Different fossils? They were separated. A mixture of marine faunas? A separation was under way. This information provided the basis for reconstructing the geography of the geological epochs (palaeogeography) in which successive generations of plants and animals evolved.

Explaining how life began

Palaeontology provided a key to one of the most mystifying of all questions: When and how did life appear on earth? The earliest known life-forms are primitive bacteria that appear as round microscopic cells in thin sections of Precambrian rock: The oldest date back some 3800 million years! About 3500 million years ago, they were living in colonies, building up layers of mineral structures (stromatolites) in marine environments so deep they allowed no oxygen and almost no light. About 1000 million years later, bacteria and single-celled blue-green algae began to release oxygen through photosynthesis. This oxygen started to accumulate in the atmosphere.

Advanced unicellular organisms with true nuclei – visible under the microscope as bigger, morphologically more complex algae – appeared about 1500 million years ago. Multicellular organisms, such as jellyfish and worms, emerged about 680 million years ago; many specimens of these soft-bodied animals were exceptionally well preserved. The earliest known vertebrates go back some 570 million years. By then, life on earth was flourishing.

Understanding the process of evolution

Evolution is the hallmark of life. But the process by which successive generations of organisms are transformed into increasingly complex forms is slow and stretched out over long periods of time. Fossils, our key to all of these evolutionary stages, have proved particularly useful in identifying 'intermediate forms'. The best-known case was the discovery of reptilian features in *Archaeopteryx,* the earliest known bird. Witness, too, the peculiar, seemingly aberrant 'mammalian reptiles' that once roamed South Africa, South America, Asia and Russia, only to die out completely in mid-Mesozoic times. Some of their features reappear in modern mammals.

Another revelation was the convergent evolution of members of genetically unrelated groups – fish, marine reptiles, mammals and diving birds – at distant moments in geological time. Note the way birds, fossil reptiles and certain modern mammals all developed wings and the ability to fly.

Scientists also saw that the evolution of certain groups (most spectacularly, the dinosaurs) was characterized by a steady increase in size.

Lastly, fossils provide evidence that a number of forms evolved very little over tens of millions of years. They are still a part of the world around us, usually represented by a lone species or genus but virtually unchanged: the gingko tree, a relic from the Carboniferous; *Lingula,* a burrowing brachiopod (a phylum of marine invertebrates) straight out of the Cambrian; its ocean-dwelling contemporary, the nautilus; and the coelacanths, survivors of an otherwise extinct fish group from the Cretaceous. These are but a few of the modern plants and animals known as 'living fossils'.

Yvette Gayrard-Valy

TIMELINE

Figures indicate millions of years ago

	Era	Period	Epoch
present		Quaternary (2–present)	Holocene (.01–present) Pleistocene (2–.01) Pliocene (7–2) Miocene (26–7) Oligocene (38–26) Eocene (54–38) Palaeocene (65–54)
	Cenozoic (65–present)	Tertiary (65–2)	
100		Cretaceous (136–65)	
200		Jurassic (193–136)	
	Mesozoic (225–65)	Triassic (225–193)	
		Permian (280–225)	
300		Carboniferous (345–280)	
400		Devonian (395–345)	
		Silurian (440–395)	
500		Ordovician (500–440)	
600	Palaeozoic (600–225)	Cambrian (600–500)	

Proterozoic (Late Precambrian Time)

FURTHER READING

Arduini, Paolo, and Giorgio Teruzzi, *Macdonald Encyclopaedia of Fossils,* 1986

Babin, Claude, *Elements of Palaeontology,* 1980

British Caenozoic Fossils, 5th edition, Trustees of the British Museum (Natural History), 1975

British Mesozoic Fossils, 5th edition, Trustees of the British Museum (Natural History), 1975

British Palaeozoic Fossils, 4th edition, Trustees of the British Museum (Natural History), 1975

Buffetaut, Eric, *A Short History of Vertebrate Palaeontology,* 1987

Carroll, Robert L., *Vertebrate Paleontology and Evolution,* 1988

———, and Colin Stearn, *Paleontology; The Record of Life,* 1989

Colbert, Edwin H., *Great Dinosaur Hunters and their Discoveries,* 1985

Cvancara, Alan M., *Sleuthing Fossils, The Art of Investigating Past Life,* 1990

Darwin, Charles R., *Origin of Species,* 1982

Desmond, Adrian J., *The Hot-Blooded Dinosaurs: A Revolution in Paleontology,* 1975

Donovan, Stephen K., *The Processes of Fossilization,* 1991

Eldredge, Niles, *Fossils: The Evolution and Extinction of Species,* 1991

———, *Life Pulse: Episodes from the Story of the Fossil Record,* 1989

Edwards, W. N., *The Early History of Palaeontology,* 1976

Faul, Henry, and Carol Faul, *It Began with a Stone: A History of Geology from the Stone Age to the Age of Plate Tectonics,* 1983

Fortey, Richard, *Fossils, The Key to the Past,* 2nd edition, 1991

Gall, J. C., *Ancient Sedimentary Environments and the Habitats of Living Organisms: Introduction to Palaeoecology,* trans. P. Wallace, 1983

Gould, Stephen Jay, *Bully for Brontosaurus: Further Reflections in Natural History,* 1992

———, *Ever Since Darwin: Reflections in Natural History,* 1991

———, *Wonderful Life: The Burgess Shale and the Nature of History,* 1990

Halstead, L. B., and Jenny Halstead, *Dinosaurs and Prehistoric Life,* 1989

Halstead, L. B., *Hunting the Past: Fossils, Rocks, Tracks and Trails, the Search for the Origin of Life,* 1982

Howard, Robert West, *The Dawnseekers: The First History of American Paleontology,* 1975

Johanson, Donald C., and Maitland A. Edey, *Lucy's Child: The Discovery of a Human Ancestor,* 1991

Lambert, David, et al., *The Cambridge Field Guide to Prehistoric Life,* 1985

Moody, Richard, *Fossils. Hamlyn Practical Guide,* 1986

Murray, John W., ed., *Atlas of Invertebrate Macrofossils,* 1985

Parker, Steve, *The Practical Paleontologist,* 1990

Pinna, Giovanni, *The Illustrated Encyclopedia of Fossils,* 1990

Pomerol, C., *Cenozoic Era: Tertiary and Quaternary,* 1982

Richter, Jean Paul, ed., *The Notebooks of Leonardo da Vinci,* 2 vols., 1970

Romer, Alfred S., *Vertebrate Paleontology,* 3rd edition, 1966

Rudwick, Martin J. S., *The Meaning of Fossils: Episodes in the History of Palaeontology,* 1972

Stanley, Steven M., *The New Evolutionary Timetable: Fossils, Genes and the Origin of Species,* 1981

Steel, R., and A.P. Harvey, *The Encyclopaedia of Prehistoric Life,* 1979

Stringer, Christopher, and Clive Gamble, *In Search of the Neanderthals: Solving the Puzzle of Human Origins,* 1993

Webster, David, *Understanding Geology,* 1987

Wendt, Herbert, *Before the Deluge,* trans. Richard Winston and Clara Winston, 1970

LIST OF ILLUSTRATIONS

The following abbreviations have been used: *a* above; *b* below; *c* centre; *l* left; *r* right; BLPV Bibliothèque du Laboratoire de Paléontologie des Vertébrés, Université de Paris-VI; MNHN Muséum National d'Histoire Naturelle, Paris; PMNH Peabody Museum of Natural History, Yale University, New Haven, Connecticut.

COVER

Front Fossil fish, Monte Bolca, northeastern Italy. Photograph. MNHN

Spine Footprints left in the mud during the Permian. Photograph. MNHN.

Back Fossil of a *Palaeortyx,* a rail-like bird from the Eocene epoch of Paris. MNHN

OPENING

1–7 Photographs in E. W. Pfizenmayer, *Mammutleichen und Urwaldmenschen in Nordost-Sibirien,* 1926. BLPV

9 Illustration from the *Petit Journal,* 9 April 1922

CHAPTER 1

CHAPTER 2

INDEX

ACKNOWLEDGMENTS

The timeline on p. 183 is adapted from *The Field Guide to Prehistoric Life*, by David Lambert and the Diagram Group, Facts on File Publications, New York, 1985.

TEXT CREDITS

Grateful acknowledgment is made for permission to use material from the following works:
(pp.130–1) Jules Verne, *Journey to the Centre of the Earth*, translated by Lowell Blair, translation © 1991 by Lowell Blair. Used by permission of Bantam Books, a division of Bantam Doubleday Dell Publishing Group, Inc.; (pp.134–5) John Fowles, *The French Lieutenant's Woman*, Jonathan Cape Ltd, 1969, © 1969 by John Fowles; (p.137) *The Notebooks of Leonardo da Vinci*, edited by Jean Paul Richter, vol.1, Dover, New York, 1970; (pp.146–9) 'Hunting Big Game of Other Days: A Boating Expedition in Search of Fossils in Alberta, Canada', by Barnum Brown, *National Geographic* Magazine, May 1919, pp. 407–29, vol. XXXV, no.5; (pp.154–5) Stephen Jay Gould, *Wonderful Life: The Burgess Shale and the Nature of History*, Hutchinson Radius, 1990, ©1989 by Stephen Jay Gould.

PHOTO CREDITS

All rights reserved 1–7, 15a, 18–9b, 44, 54, 62–3, 66, 68–9, 69r, 70b, 86–7, 88–9, 91b, 97, 104a, 113, 115, 123, 126b, 130, 131, 181. American Museum of Natural History, New York 96, 107,Archiv für Kunst und Geschichte, Berlin 108–11. Archives Gallimard, Paris 31a, 31b, 64a, 95b, 139, 162, 184, 189. B. Battail, Paris 174. Bibliothèque de l'Institut, Paris 63a. Bibliothèque du Muséum National d'Histoire Naturelle, Paris 24–5b, 27, 30, 32–3, 33b, 38, 39, 40–3, 52, 53b, 57a, 57b, 60–1, 62, 67, 71a, 79b, 80-1, 82, 101, 102b, 103, 132–3, 164–5. Bibliothèque Municipale, Hyères 60a, 61a. Bibliothèque Nationale, Paris 24–5a, 29a, 32, 34a, 35, 36, 37b, 46, 47, 48–51, 70a, 84–5, 100, 128, 129, 138r, 143, 162, 166–7, 171. Bridgeman Art Library, London 78, 81. Charmet, Paris 9, 58, 59, 112, 124–5. Dagli Orti 16, 17, 56. Edimédia, Paris 144, 164l. ET Archive 85, 102a. Mary Evans/Explorer, Paris 23a, 90a, 90–1, 98b, 99, 104b, 106, 114, 126–7. Explorer Archives, Paris 79a. Giraudon 24, 28, 55, 65. Institut Royal des Sciences Naturelles de Belgique, Brussels 83, 92a, 92–3, 94. Keystone 98a. S. Laroche, Paris 170, 171–3. Mansell Collection, London 90b. Musée de l'Homme, Paris 12a, 12b, 13. Musée des Arts et Traditions Populaires, Paris 45. National Museum of Wales, Cardiff 15b, 22a. Novosti, Paris 127b. P.P.P., Paris 175. Peabody Museum, Yale University, New Haven, Connecticut 118–9a, 118–9b, 120, 121. Peale Museum, Baltimore 116–7. Rapho 21b, 105. Scala, Florence 20–1a, 26, 37a. D. Serrette, Muséum National d'Histoire Naturelle, Paris front cover, back cover, spine, 10, 22b, 53a, 72–7, 148, 156–61, 176–7, 180. Staatliche Kunstsammlungen, Dresden 23b. Tallandier, Paris 140. P. Taquet, Paris 163, 178–9. Jean Vigne, Paris 28–9b. Viollet, Paris 11, 18–9a, 34b, 64–5, 71b, 122, 136, 138l, 145, 149, 168, 169. Yorkshire Museum, York 14.

Yvette Gayrard-Valy
research engineer at the French National Centre
for Scientific Research (CNRS), is currently assigned
to the Palaeontological Institute of the National Museum
of Natural History in Paris, where she is in charge of invertebrate collections.
When she is not assisting
researchers, she is busy preparing exhibitions,
delivering lectures and writing books and articles
that make palaeontology
more accessible to the general public.

For Cécile

© 1987 Gallimard

English translation © Thames and Hudson Ltd, London,
and Harry N. Abrams, Inc., New York, 1994

Translated from the French by I. Mark Paris

British Library Cataloguing-in-Publication Data

A catalogue record for this book is available from
the British Library

ISBN 0–500–30039–9

Printed and bound in Italy
by Editoriale Libraria, Trieste